The Light Within the Light

THE LIGHT
WITHIN
THE LIGHT

Portraits of Donald Hall, Richard Wilbur,

Maxine Kumin, and Stanley Kunitz

BY JEANNE BRAHAM

engravings by Barry Moser

DAVID R. GODINE · *Publisher*

BOSTON

First published in 2007 by
DAVID R. GODINE · *Publisher*
Post Office Box 450
Jaffrey, New Hampshire 03452
www.godine.com

LIBRARY OF CONGRESS CATALOGING-IN-PUBLICATION DATA
Braham, Jeanne, 1940–
The light within the light : portraits of Donald Hall, Richard Wilbur,
Maxine Kumin, and Stanley Kunitz / by Jeanne Braham ;
with engravings by Barry Moser.
p.   cm.
Includes bibliographical references.
ISBN 1-56792-316-X (alk. paper)
1. Poets, American—20th century—Biography.
2.Poets, American—Homes and haunts—New England.
3. Hall, Donald, 1928–   4. Wilbur, Richard, 1921–
5. Kumin, Maxine, 1925–   6. Kunitz, Stanley, 1905–2006.
7. American poetry—New England—History
and criticism.   8. New England—In literature.
9. Light and darkness in literature.   I. Title.
PS323.5.B68   2007
811'.5409—dc22
2006023669

FIRST EDITION
Printed in the United States of America

Contents

Introduction

IN THE LATE SPRING OF 1962 Robert Frost came to speak at the dedication of the new library at the College of Wooster in Ohio. I was in the audience that evening, straining with the rest of the eager undergraduates to hear what the old master (he would die the following year at the age of eighty-nine) had to say. An English major at Wooster and marching in an unimaginative line resolutely toward graduate school, I supposed that Crane's, Auden's, and Eliot's ironic poems lay much closer to my sensibility than Frost's. Moreover, in his late years Frost had become a stage performer: a crusty, avuncular New England philosopher-king who courted and crooned to his audiences. I expected to be entertained rather than riveted.

Frost ambled on stage assisted by the faculty dean who, after pinning a lapel microphone to Frost's dark suit jacket, retired stage left. Turning his Old Man of the Mountain face toward the audience and leaning toward us as if he had something conspiratorial to share, Frost began to speak his poems. I was riveted. I remember he intoned "Fire and Ice" and "Desert Places" in a voice terrifyingly devoid of emotion. "Stopping by Woods on a Snowy Evening," a poem that seemed harmless to me as a youngster, turned sinister, especially as Frost cadenced those last two repeating lines, "And miles to go before I sleep / And miles to go before I sleep" into a kind of existential mantra. It was an evening I've never forgotten, for it reminded me of poetry's power to strip us clean of our expectations and to find, in the clearing, new and startling revelations.

Although the quartet of poets who appear in these pages

knew Frost, some as a friend, some as a teacher at Amherst College or Harvard College, some as the paterfamilias of the Bread Loaf Writers Conference, only Richard Wilbur claims him as a major literary influence. Stanley Kunitz sought some of his inspiration in the English mystic poet and engraver William Blake, Maxine Kumin admired the poems of W. H. Auden, while Donald Hall loved the sound and form of the poems of Thomas Hardy. Their own rich assortment of contemporaries, whose careers began to blossom after World War II, also contributed to their poetic development: Robert Lowell, John Berryman, James Wright, William Stafford, Mona Van Duyn, Philip Booth, Adrienne Rich, Theodore Roethke, Denise Levertov, Galway Kinnell, Anne Sexton, Louis Simpson, W. S. Merwin, Robert Bly, Carolyn Kizer, Gerald Stern.

Yet they bear, in individual and collective ways, the imprint of Frost's legacy: a New England landscape that is not simply the nominal setting for a poem, but an emotional and psychological context contributing to the poem's momentum and message; a clear commitment to form, without which writing poetry would be, in Frost's words, "like playing tennis without a net"; and the belief that a poem is not didactic, but rather a vehicle providing an immediate visceral experience, one that proceeds out of its own inevitabilities or, as Frost would put it, riding like "a piece of ice on a hot stove. . . on its own melting."

Why select these four poets from the ranks of the several dozen first-rate poets writing in our country today? Besides the fact that they have garnered a gymnasium full of literary prizes – Pulitzers, National Book Awards, Fulbrights, Guggenheims – and have been state and national poet laureates – they display a daunting range and an undeviating commitment to supporting and strengthening the arts that stretches over five decades. In addition to their primary medium of poetry, their work includes short stories, novels, memoirs, children's books, essays, translations, and lyrics for Broadway musicals. They have taught or mentored four decades of younger poets and writers, established work centers, sponsored prizes, judged literary awards, and supported and strengthened community outreach programs in the arts. They cast a wide light.

As poets who have lived through World War II (Wilbur and Kunitz served in the military), Korea, Viet Nam, and the U.S. military involvements in the Middle East, the Balkans, Afghanistan, and Iraq, they write in nuanced ways about the complexities of moral choice in the modern world and the equally complex role of the poet as witness. In a world conditioned by prepackaged news or reports "spun" by master spinners from one camp or another, their poems deliver truer news than we're accustomed to getting.

And perhaps most appealingly to me, their poems are bound to a landscape, a corner of New England imbued with a spirit that is both of the place and of the poet. To climb with Kumin beyond the horse barn and enormous garden to the high pasture she named The Elysian Field, to jog with Wilbur's young boys through a pasture in Cummington where their barking dog startles out a pheasant, to follow Kunitz down to the sea to view the sad spectacle of the dying Wellfleet whale, to walk with Hall and the (immortal) dog Gus up New Canada Road under the paperbark birches is to enter the world via a unique perception, one that has never existed before in quite that way, one that will never exist again in quite that way. This world, this way of seeing is preserved by the alchemy of the creative act into a vessel we can drink from again and again.

In the much-loved poem titled "How Poetry Comes to Me," Gary Snyder describes the mysterious interplay between poet and poem in this way:

> It comes blundering over the
> Boulders at night, it stays
> Frightened outside the
> Range of my campfire

> *I go to meet it at the*
> *Edge of the light.*

Perhaps because of New England's harsh climate and famously dark winter, its poets explore the "edge of the light" more than most. From the Puritan allegorical debates pitting the light of moral rectitude against the dark of moral chaos, to Dickinson's efforts to "Grow Accustomed to the Dark," to Frost's narrators who claim to be "Acquainted with the Night," the narrators in many New England-situated poems find themselves surrounded by a dark world, one set in startling juxtaposition to the "clearing" a poem makes. That circle of light assumes its definition in a complicated dance with the dark.

    If the act of creating a poem makes a clearing in the dark, there is another glow embedded within the poem, the light within the light, the long half life of the poem's impact on the reader. Against the backdrop of a dark world, Donald Hall, Richard Wilbur, Maxine Kumin, and Stanley Kunitz create poems that are illumined from within, holding a vision of human possibility steady in the light.

JEANNE BRAHAM

Donald Hall

BLUE GHOST

Donald Hall

Eagle Pond Farm, the familial farmhouse, New Hampshire acreage and pond resting in the lap of Mount Kearsarge and lovingly rendered in Donald Hall's poems and memoirs, seems to belong to another century – a time when sugaring was accomplished tree by tree, pail by pail, when draft horses skidded logs out of the perpendicular woodlot behind the farmhouse, and when the country kitchen was such a bustling hub it required its own door. It is the home of Donald Hall, and before that the home of his mother and maternal grandparents, Kate and Wesley Wells, and before that Kate's parents, generations immortalized in books like *String Too Short to be Saved* and *Seasons at Eagle Pond*. In short stories, essays, memoirs, children's books, and particularly in fifteen volumes of poems, Hall has excavated the geographical, psychological, and emotional landscape of what it means to "be home."

And indeed, the farmhouse materializes, close to a curve in Wilmot, looking almost exactly as it does in the 1904 photo that appears on the cover of *String Too Short to be Saved* – a twelve-room house designed to accommodate multiple generations under the same roof, white clapboard exterior, double windows with dark green wooden shutters, and the wide welcoming, south-facing side porch with doors into the living room and kitchen. South of the house is an unpainted barn with several connected sheds and beyond that, a stone retaining wall, seeming to hold back Ragged Mountain as it rises steeply to the northwest. Across the road is Eagle Pond, which would qualify as a lake by most people's estimates. Twenty-five acres in size, muddy at the edges and deep in the middle, its waters fed an eagle twice daily during Hall's great-grandfather's time.

Donald Hall is tall – well over six feet, bearded, unstooped, and clearly entertained by the antics of his five-month-old tabby and tortoise-shell kitties, Thelma and Louise. He has the habit of looking out over the top of his wire-rim glasses, eyes twinkling, surveying the moment for its possibilities, grave or humorous. The living room, with its wide-plank painted floors and walls lined with books, contains the Glenwood stove that figures prominently in many of his recollections of boyhood experiences at the farm, and Hall's reading chair and lamp are positioned so that he can look out the window and see Kearsarge, rising in the distance.

Many poetry lovers know the story of Hall's radical decision to give up tenure at the University of Michigan and return to his grandparents' farmhouse where he and his second wife, the poet Jane Kenyon, lived and wrote in solitude and in communion for twenty years – until her untimely death at the age of forty-seven, a victim of a virulent form of leukemia.

Hall observes that even though he and Jane transplanted their daily lives to New Hampshire in January of 1976, in fact he had chronicled the summers he spent as a boy at Eagle Pond, the memories of this vivid landscape and colorful cast of characters, in memoirs and poems for years before they made the move. Eagle Pond Farm and the "blue ghost" of Mount Kearsarge, rising five miles to the south, have always been his "true subject."

> I began writing about New Hampshire as early as the age of sixteen in my first published poem. I wrote *String Too Short to be Saved*, the memoir about my grandparents and my boyhood summers at Eagle Pond Farm, when I was thirty. So even though I might have been physically at Harvard, or Oxford, or California, or Ann Arbor, I was living emotionally in New Hampshire. I think I told myself that I was writing about New Hamp-

shire so much because I was unable to be there; I thought I had to retrieve and reconstitute it in memoirs and in poems. In fact when Janie and I decided to move here I remember saying to her, "I doubt that I'll write about New Hampshire any more." I've written endlessly about it.

Had Jane not loved it here, I think I would have been too cautious to make the move. At that time I had child support to pay, one child in college and another about ready to go to college. Was this really the time to quit my job, lose my salary, lose my benefits? Part of me thought that was insane.

Jane, on the other hand, was the child of musician parents. They were freelancers, living from job to job. It seemed natural to her that I could do that also. And I found that I could – working flat out all the time. Sometimes I got into a panic about where the next tuition payment would come from, or the next mortgage check, and at times like those I'd take on a project I otherwise wouldn't have considered – like a thousand-page, multiple-genre anthology widely used as a college textbook. Or I worked sometimes for a publication called the *Ford Times*, a magazine that ran articles about the merits of Ford cars. I remember once writing a piece about Gertrude Stein and her love for the Ford automobile.

Jane adored the place and she found that her work grew and deepened after we left the confines of the academic world and entered the riskier and more energizing world of Eagle Pond Farm. I think we both felt an exhilaration in being here.

Of course, I had a whole storehouse of memories and images from boyhood summers spent in this place. I was the only grandchild of two sets of grandparents, a boy not much interested in his peers but fascinated with the "old people" up here who were wonderful storytellers. I loved to hear them talk and tried to think up questions that would prompt more stories.

My grandfather, the farmer Wesley Wells, was at the emotional center of this place and my life. He loved to tell stories full of colorful details; he was also a reciter of poems. And he loved it that he had in me someone who was a good audience. In the summers I spent here as a boy I'd get up to feed the chickens quite early and while my grandfather went to cut hay, I'd return to my bedroom (the room I use as my study now) and work on my poems. After lunch he and I would hay together. On Sundays visitors and relatives came and they, too, told stories. So some of the patterns I love were set in me quite early: a life that is solitary and communal, a love for language – its rhythms and tonalities, and a love for old people and their richly layered stories. So when I returned to this place I was not only coming "home," I was coming home to language: the cadences, the shapely narratives, the characteristic turns of humor that carry so much in the way of possibility.

When I lived in Ann Arbor, my sense of time was very different. . . . I never seemed to be content to live in the present moment. Most of the time I found myself thinking, "Well, maybe I can take a sabbatical next year and live in England," or "Five years from now I can go. . . ." My father died at the age of fifty-two; he worked at a job he did not love and he longed to retire – but then he died. That's probably a common story in America, but I was wary, fearful that it could happen to me.

When I was in New Hampshire less than a year I suddenly noticed that I was living in the present for the first time in my life. I looked forward to each day, not to some trip I was going to make six months from now. Time really changed for me and I realized that the change hinged on happiness.

Born in New Haven, Connecticut, in 1928, Hall was the only child of Donald Andrew Hall and his wife Lucy. Educated at Phillips Exeter in New Hampshire and subsequently at Harvard, Oxford, and Stanford Universities, he began writing as an adolescent. His fascination with sound in poems drew him initially to the work of Edgar Allan Poe. "I also liked him because he was spooky and because I, too, wanted to be obsessed, addicted, and cursed."

He continued to write throughout his prep school days at Exeter and, although only sixteen years old, attended the Bread Loaf Writers Conference where he met the poet Robert Frost, one of the four towering literary figures he would later explore in a memoir originally titled *Remembering Poets: Reminiscences and Opinions*. (In addition to Frost, the memoir portrays Hall's encounters with T. S. Eliot, Ezra Pound, and Dylan Thomas.) Though he didn't talk to Frost about his own fledgling poems while at Bread Loaf, he remembers talking about poetry with him on the porch of the old wooden inn outside Middlebury, Vermont, and sharing a game of softball that was "less than graceful."

While an undergraduate at Harvard he served on the editorial board of the *Harvard Advocate* and mingled with a group of young writers who, like him, were poised to accomplish significant work in the literary world: John Ashbery; Robert Bly – who remains his closest friend – Frank O'Hara; Adrienne Rich, whom he dated briefly; and John Ciardi, "that master of barbed wit, who was my first teacher at Harvard. Bill Merwin and Galway Kinnell were at Princeton at the same time. It was just a Golden Age for poets."

> We talked and argued poetry all the time. And there was another group of poets just a bit older than I, in and around the Boston area – like Richard Wilbur; when I returned to Harvard as a Junior Fellow three years later, I came to know Wilbur better, as well as

John Holmes and Philip Booth. Robert Lowell was
around at that time too. These were very exciting years.

After graduating from Harvard, Hall went to Oxford to study
for two years. During that time he not only won the university's prestigious Newdigate Prize, but he also became poetry
editor of the *Paris Review*. After returning to the United States
and spending a year as a creative writing fellow at Stanford, he
returned to Harvard where he spent three years as a junior fellow in the Society of Fellows. Junior fellows, as Hall explains it,
can be appointed from any discipline and spend three years
"doing what they please." "The Society consists of ten senior
fellows – professors largely, from various fields, whose duties
are dinner and the election of new junior fellows – and about
twenty-four junior fellows. . . . At my first dinner I sat next to a
young man and asked him what he did. "Mathematical linguis-
tics," he said, to my bewilderment; I had met Noam Chomsky."[1]

He was appointed to the faculty of the University of Michigan in 1957 and continued to teach there until 1975. Three
years after he married Jane Kenyon they made their momen-
tous move to Eagle Pond Farm.

MOUNT KEARSARGE

Great blue mountain! Ghost.
I look at you
from the porch of the farmhouse
where I watched you all summer
as a boy. Steep sides, narrow flat
patch on top –
you are clear to me
like the memory of one day.
Blue! Blue!
the top of the mountain floats
in haze.

I will not rock on this porch
when I am old. I turn my back on you,
Kearsarge, I close
my eyes, and you rise inside me,
blue ghost.

This was a poem written – yes – about the mountain right outside this window, but it was written when I didn't live here, when I thought I never could.

I loved the place, of course. My grandmother was born here, my mother was born here, but I thought after my grandmother died that I'd never drive by this house again. My mother had a little money, but her sisters, my aunts, had very little money. The farm was their capital. I couldn't imagine how I could ever come to own it, to arrange a mortgage on the place. But we all worked out a way to do it. The first winter we were here, January of 1976, we earned our stripes; the house had no insulation, no central heat. This twelve-room house dwindled to a one-room house with a kitchen sometimes habitable. Working at the dining room table twenty feet from the Glenwood I felt chilly. The next summer we added aluminum storms and screens and some insulation, and we also added two more wood-stoves, one for each study, so that we could each work regardless of the weather.

I've come to understand after being here for some time that this place has become a centering place for me. The culture – or maybe the feelings I had toward the culture and the old people here when I was a boy – have created a platform for me from which to view the rest of the world. It's my vantage point. And Kearsarge represents that for me. For two hundred years the people of this house have looked south to Kearsarge at dawn and at dusk to tell the coming weather, to get their bearings. Kearsarge is as good a predictor now as it was in 1803 when these south windows were put in.

Perhaps because of the pressures of freelancing or perhaps because of his dedicated work habits, Hall has been staggeringly prolific. He has produced fifteen volumes of poems, four plays, and more than twenty books of prose – children's books, books on baseball, personal essays, short stories, literary criticism, and textbooks. He suggests that, in any given year, it has not been unusual to publish a book of essays, a volume of poems, and a play or a children's book. For years, his work habits have included rising around 4:30 or 5 A.M., working first on poetry ("because it is the hardest"), then on multiple other projects until noon; then, with occasional breaks, he spends the rest of the day reading, revising (it is not uncommon for poems to go through eighty to one hundred drafts), and proofing. In the evening he watches baseball (or basketball or football) via satellite dish, while dictating some of the several thousand letters he writes each year. *Life Work*, a memoir chronicling the work patterns and daily routines at Eagle Pond Farm, underscores the energizing nature of these work habits. He quotes with relish sculptor Henry Moore's response when Hall asked him to describe, on the occasion of his eightieth birthday, what he thought was the secret of life. "With anyone else the answer would have begin with an ironic laugh," Hall says,

> but Henry Moore answered me straight: the secret of life is to have a task, something you devote your entire life to, something you bring everything to, every minute of the day for your whole life. And the most important thing is – it must be something you cannot possibly do.[2]
>
> I saw Henry Moore absolutely lost in the love of what his hands could do – and it made me think of the pleasure I have at my desk, creating, revising. I can get

absolutely lost in the work. It's bliss – to be lost inside
your task, loosening yourself into the work that you love.
I love my work so much it is as if I do not work at all.

The decision to live in rural New Hampshire, to "fit into" a
community and a culture utterly unlike that of Harvard or
Oxford or Ann Arbor, might have served up hefty challenges
for some. Hall acknowledges that he is probably still perceived
as an outsider, a suburbanite, someone not born and bred in
New Hampshire and living in a home that has "a lot more
books in it than, say, cans of applesauce," but he believes he's
accepted as an integral part of the community because he loves
it so clearly. Soon after they arrived, he and Jane became regular churchgoers in the South Danbury Christian Church down
the road where Hall's grandmother played the organ for sev-
enty-eight years (from the age of fourteen to the age of ninety-
two). And although he's often been on the road doing poetry
readings – to places as distant as China and India, he is also a
recognizable presence at Wilmot and Danbury community
gatherings, a very popular reader locally.

> I include in my writing a lot of things that neighbors
> and friends tell me, things that embody the rhythms of
> local speech and the light of humor and insight. So, as
> long as I don't patronize or pretend to know what I do
> not know, as long as I don't take myself too solemnly,
> I think I become a kind of spokesman – a writer who
> takes very seriously the task of preserving a certain cut
> of character. The portrait I created of my grandfather
> in memoirs and poems, the way he spoke, moved, the
> relationship he had with his horses, is one example of
> that kind of preservation. For after all, that kind of char-
> acter, that way of being in the world is diminishing –
> or at least it grows more attenuated here in New

Hampshire. When I read around here, people expect to
hear "Mount Kearsarge" and "Names of Horses." If I
fail to read those poems, I hear about it.[3]

NAMES OF HORSES

All winter your brute shoulders strained against collars, padding
and steerhide over the ash hames, to haul
sledges of cordwood for drying through spring and summer,
for the Glenwood stove next winter, and for the simmering range.

In April you pulled cartloads of manure to spread on the fields,
dark manure of Holsteins, and the knobs of your own clustered with oats.
All summer you mowed the grass in meadow and hayfield,
*   the mowing machine*
clacketing beside you, while the sun walked high in the morning;

and after noon's heat, you pulled a clawed rake through the same acres,
gathering stacks, and dragged the wagon from stack to stack,
and the built hayrack back, uphill to the chaffy barn,
three loads of hay a day, hanging wide from the hayrack.

Sundays you trotted the two miles to church with the light load
of a leather quartertop buggy, and grazed in the sound of hymns.
Generation on generation, your neck rubbed the window sill
of the stall, smoothing the wood as the sea smooths glass.

When you were old and lame, when your shoulders hurt bending to graze,
one October the man who fed you and kept you, and harnessed you
*   every morning,*
led you through the corn stubble to sandy ground above Eagle Pond,
and dug a hole beside you where you stood shuddering in your skin,

and lay the shotgun's muzzle in the boneless hollow behind your ear,
and fired the slug into your brain, and felled you into your grave,

shoveling sand to cover you, setting goldenrod upright above you,
where by next summer a dent in the ground made your monument.

For a hundred and fifty years, in the pasture of dead horses,
roots of pine trees pushed through the pale curves of your ribs,
yellow blossoms flourished above you in autumn, and in winter
frost heaved your bones in the ground – old toilers, soil makers:

O Roger, Mackerel, Riley, Ned, Nellie, Chester, Lady Ghost.

When I was young I thought maybe the old didn't see,
didn't relish the beauty they lived in. Then I learned:
For more than a hundred years, anybody willing to
leave this countryside has been rewarded for leaving it
by more money, leisure, and creature comforts. A few
may have stayed from fecklessness or lack of gumption;
more have stayed from family feeling or homesickness;
but most stay from love . . . . We are self-selected place-
lovers. There's no reason to live here except for love.[4]

Hall has a deep and sonorous voice, one well-trained to
reach the back of a room without amplification. When he reads
or speaks lines from his poems from memory, he emphasizes
the internal cadences, the slant rhymes and assonance in the
words, sometimes unconsciously conducting with his right
hand as if he hears with an inner ear the music of his own
making.

Convinced that poems "are pleasure first," that the words
and sounds of a poem appeal first to the senses, give joy even
before they yield meaning, he believes that we read poetry not
simply with the eye, but with the ear – and especially with the
mouth.

Sound was my doorway into poems and I believe you
taste sounds. You chew on them. And they are delicious.

When I read poems, just sitting silently here in my chair, I can feel the muscles of my throat working. Poets read poems better than actors, you know. Poets speak the voice of the poem – which is far more complicated than distilling out what "it means." For example, I think sound – particularly vowel sound – is vital to elegiac poetry and I've come to realize that I write a lot of elegiac poetry, poetry that tries to preserve and honor a way of life, poetry that tries to keep the dead around.[5]

Maybe that comes from experiencing loss at an early age. I think I was about nine years old when three of my great aunts and uncles died within a single year of cancer. My father died in early middle age and my mother's parents whom I loved so much were old when I was a boy. So from an early age I was well aware of mortality.

I wrote the poem "My Son, My Executioner" when I was twenty-five and my first child, Andrew, was born. I remember being shocked by this feeling that my replacement had arrived.

I was worried about what my son would think about this poem when he grew up. When he was about fourteen he said to me, "That poem really wasn't about you and me. That was about you and your father.[6]

MY SON, MY EXECUTIONER

My son, my executioner
  I take you in my arms
Quiet and small and just astir
  And whom my body warms.

Sweet death, small son, our instrument
  Of immortality,

Your cries and hungers document
Our bodily decay.

We twenty-five and twenty-two,
Who seemed to live forever,
Observe enduring life in you
And start to die together.

In 1989, when he was sixty-one, Hall was diagnosed with colon cancer. Surgery followed, but by 1992 cancer reappeared in his liver. He underwent another operation plus chemotherapy, though he was told that his odds of living another five years were slim. Then, in early 1994, when Kenyon and Hall were concentrating on his complete recovery, hoping against hope that his cancer would not return, she awoke with a severe nosebleed and subsequently was diagnosed with a rare, difficult-to-treat form of leukemia that took her life fifteen months later at the age of forty-seven, leaving Hall with a palpable grief, apparent to this day.

Hall became her caregiver during her illness, all the while working feverishly on his twelfth volume of poems, *The Old Life*. A bone marrow transplant in Seattle had provided Kenyon a new immune system and some hope, but within six months the old cancer cells overcame the new marrow and there was nothing left to do. After Kenyon's death, Hall wrote a fiercely personal set of elegies titled *Without*, poems that interweave memories of deep and abiding love with nearly unbearable loss. In one of his most moving elegies, "Weeds and Peonies," he walks restlessly in the garden Kenyon loved to tend, remembering her special affection for the heavy blossoming peonies planted by the porch of the farmhouse. Watching as their giant petals blow across the abandoned garden, he looks up and imagines Kenyon vanishing into the snowflakes, into the image of Kearsarge in the distance. He recalls the words he spoke

when she went off for a day of climbing on the mountain:
"Hurry back."

WEEDS AND PEONIES

Your peonies burst out, white as snow squalls,
with red flecks at their shaggy centers
in your border of prodigies by the porch.
I carry one magnanimous blossom indoors
and float it in a glass bowl, as you used to do.

Ordinary pleasures, contentment recollected,
blow like snow into the abandoned garden,
overcoming the daisies. Your blue coat
vanishes down Pond Road into imagined snowflakes
with Gus at your side, his great tail swinging,

but you will not reappear, tired and satisfied,
and grief's repeated particles suffuse the air —
like the dog yipping through the entire night,
or the cat stretching awake, then curling
as if to dream of her mother's milky nipples.

A raccoon dislodged a geranium from its pot.
Flowers, roots, and dirt lay upended
in the back garden where the lilies begin
their daily excursions above stone walls
in the season of old roses. I pace beside weeds

and snowy peonies, staring at Mount Kearsarge
where you climbed wearing purple hiking boots.
"Hurry back. Be careful, climbing down."
Your peonies lean their vast heads westward
as if they might topple. Some topple.

Perhaps because of the popular PBS documentary Bill Moyers filmed about Kenyon and Hall's life together, perhaps because of their habit of reading together at poetry festivals, or perhaps because images of their life together "in double solitude and communion" began to appear in so many of their poems, it generated its own legend. Donald Hall's work and Jane Kenyon's work are, increasingly, being talked about in tandem.[7]

> I do think it's very likely that our work will be considered together in the future. In fact, some are already writing about us as a pair. We have our papers together in the Special Collections Archives at the University of New Hampshire in Durham, and I would suppose that writers will look at us as a matched set, a team perhaps, two poets working steadily side by side. But I hope that doesn't happen in my lifetime. I've rejected all suggestions of biography or collected letters. After I'm dead, I doubt that I will interfere.
>
> In the early years we spent together, our work was often compared, usually to Jane's detriment. That simply wasn't fair. After all, Jane was first my student and her development as a poet – and certainly her recognition as a poet – came slowly at first.
>
> When we first came out here we had been married for only three years and she concentrated on her reading and writing. Then one day Bob Bly came out to visit. He read some of her stuff, and he barked, "You need a master." Jane replied that she didn't want a male model, that she wanted a mistress rather than a master. Bly suggested the Russian poet, Anna Akhmatova. It was a wonderful suggestion and at first she started to compare various translations of Akhmatova poems, then located a Russian speaker and began working on her own translations. She translated and published six

Akhmatova poems in her first volume of poetry (1978) and many more in *Twenty Poems of Anna Akhmatova* in 1980. That marked a real turning point for Jane. As a result of her close readings of Akhmatova she could explore the myriad possibilities of the brief lyric, particularly Akhmatova's habit of offering up a surprise ending. And of course it was the brief, intense lyric that Jane perfected for the rest of her writing life.

I think she was writing her very best poems at the time she died. She was at the top of her form. At forty-seven Jane was much better than I was at forty-seven, and who knows what she might have written had she lived. When I think about this, her death seems, freshly, an outrage.

Despite the grief, despite the rage, work sustains and energizes. "If work is not an antidote to death, nor a denial of it, death is a powerful stimulus to work: Get done what you can," Hall says (in *Life Work*) with the ring of conviction. *The Painted Bed*, a collection of poems published in 2002, followed Without. In 2003 he published *Breakfast Served Any Time All Day*, a collection of essays about poetry. A new collection of stories, *Willow Temple*, also appeared in 2003, and Hall has completed a memoir of his life with Jane titled *The Best Day The Worst Day*. A recently published poem titled "Witness" appearing in the December 31, 2003, issue of the *New York Times*, underscores the rich and unsettling history through which Hall has lived.

It's a poem about old age, about remembrance, about being a witness to so much in the last century. I remember as a child sitting on the couch and listening to Edward R. Murrow on the radio, describing London burning and I began to think about this arc of history: from World War II to 9/11 to Iraq. As a poet it's not my obligation to take a political position. But as a citizen I have views, I have feelings, and they will come out. I feel my responsibility as a citizen, as a human being to speak my mind when our government is leading us in the wrong direction.

Poetry isn't, after all, a bully pulpit, a place to preach. It's not even a forum for sharing information. It operates in a different way, as a location where the emotions of being human can be put out, can be received. Poetry allows readers to exercise their own emotional possibilities through the words of others. And I think there is also comfort in this latest poem, a certain balance in acknowledging the whole arc of history to which I am a witness.

And so there is. After a long meditative night filled with recollections of world history and personal history, the "witness" sets out at sunrise for the morning paper, knowing all too well that he will encounter in its pages more news of a destructive world. Yet, "In the rearview/ mirror the sky over Kearsarge is pink, lavender, and orange" and Kearsarge is there, a model of survival and endurance, as is the witness.

ENDNOTES

1. To read more about Hall's early years in England, at Stanford, and at Harvard, see *Remembering Poets: Reminiscences and Opinions* (1978), or the revised and expanded edition titled *Their Ancient Glittering Eyes* (1992).

2. Donald Hall, *Life Work* (Boston: Beacon, 1993), pp. 51–54. Hall describes here his warm friendship with the sculptor, Henry Moore. He has also written a book about Henry Moore titled *Henry Moore: The Life and Work of a Great Sculptor* (1966).

3. Hall's love for Eagle Pond Farm is detailed in a variety of collections of prose, poetry, and children's books, including *String Too Short to be Saved: Recollections of Summer on a New England Farm* (1961, with an expanded edition appearing in 1979), *Seasons at Eagle Pond* (1987), *Here at Eagle Pond* (1992), *Life*

Work (1993), *The Farm Summer, 1942* (1994), *Lucy's Christmas* (1994), and *Lucy's Summer* (1995).

4. Hall, *Seasons at Eagle Pond* (Boston and New York: Houghton Mifflin Company, 1987), 84.

5. Hall has written extensively about sound, form, and syntax in his poetry and prose. See particularly *Goatfoot Milktongue Twinbird: Interviews, Essays, and Notes on Poetry, 1970–76* (1978); *Death to the Death of Poetry: Essays, Reviews, Notes, Interviews* (1994); and *Breakfast Served Any Time All Day* (2003).

6. Bill Moyers, *The Language of Life* (New York: Doubleday, 1995), 151. Moyers's best-selling *The Language of Life* contains in-depth interviews with Donald Hall and Jane Kenyon. Moyers also produced a PBS documentary on Hall and Kenyon titled *A Life Together*. Steven Ratiner's book, *Giving Their Word: Conversations with Contemporary Poets* (Amherst: University of Massachusetts Press, 2002), contains two fascinating interviews with Hall, one prior to, and one after Jane Kenyon's death. Allan Reeder's interview for the October 1996 *Atlantic Monthly* explores the impact of Kenyon's death in Hall's recent work. Poignant portraits of Hall and Kenyon appear in essays by poet and then neighbor, Wesley McNair, in *Mapping the Heart: Reflections on Place and Poetry* (Pittsburgh: Carnegie Mellon University Press, 2003).

Richard Wilbur

A DIFFICULT BALANCE

Richard Wilbur

P AST THE CUMMINGTON FAIRGROUNDS and opposite the Joyners' Dairy Farm" are two of the coordinates Richard Wilbur offers when locating his eighty-acre property in the foothills of the Berkshires. The western Massachusetts landscape is one of rolling hills, open pasture lands, stone walls, and small streams meandering into the nearby Westfield River.

When my wife Charlee and I were courting, we once drove through this area in my roommate's car, on our way to a football game at Williams College. We actually did remark, "We must get back here someday." And that day came in the middle sixties when we wanted to escape the oppressive summers in Middletown, Connecticut. We decided to look for a "little cabin" up north. In 1965 we bought the "little cabin" and fifty acres around it; with that came a ruined Olympic-sized swimming pool, a burned-out house foundation, and a ruined tennis court. At first, we spent our summers here. And after a while we just liked it so well we decided to build a house on that leftover foundation.

For a time we thought about making the swimming pool into a rose garden. That was actually a serious consideration. But we found that putting the right kind of soil into a pool of that size would be terribly expensive; we compromised and put in a small pool. On the site of a ruined tennis court my son Nathan and I, all of one

July, took out nineteen tons of broken-up reinforced
concrete and got asphalt poured in its place, making a
usable tennis court. Nathan was fifteen when we moved
here and we had a very young son, Aaron. Our oldest
child, Ellen, was off at Bennington and our oldest son,
Christopher, was headed for Harvard by that time.

Wilbur worked for many years in a distinctive two-story silo on
the property.

Arthur Miller had built such a structure on his Connecticut estate, and he advised me to apply to the
Unadilla Silo Company if I wanted one built here. They
kindly designed a double-walled silo with a twenty-four-
foot diameter; the double wall was for insulation, and
the diameter was large so that bookshelves and furni-
ture could be accommodated. A curving stair ran up
the wall from the front door to the second floor. A
Franklin stove did most of my heating, and the first
floor was used for storage. There were several windows
and a window seat on the second floor. The tornado
which, in the mid-1990s, wiped out the Great Barring-
ton fairgrounds made a local stop in Cummington and
smashed my tower.

Somewhat later, a neighbor, David Gowdy, designed a handsome work studio for Wilbur. The space is divided into two
large, bright workrooms, fronted by an entry wall hung with
posters from the musical Candide (for which he wrote the lyrics)
and from many productions of his translations of Molière and
Racine. The room to the left is clearly his writing space, domi-
nated by a large desk, and swivel chair, its walls lined with
books. A sofa and several upholstered chairs are arranged in
the other space, an area designed for conversations, interviews,

collaborative meetings. Although the studio is a stone's throw from the house, it is intensely private space, and the silence is penetrated only when Charlee buzzes Wilbur from the house for an unavoidable phone call.

Well over six feet tall, dark haired and broad shouldered, Richard Wilbur speaks and moves with the same measured grace that characterizes his poetry. In a deep baritone voice he enunciates words with the precision of an elocution instructor, yet he often interrupts his perfectly parsed sentences with a booming laugh.

> Philip Burton, a man of the theater, once called my speech "Mid-Atlantic" – halfway between British and American speech patterns, I suppose he meant. My habit of projecting my voice came from two things, I think: more than half a century of giving poetry readings and years in the classroom, where I tried to read Milton and others aloud in a manner worthy of them. No teacher has a right to mutter Milton.

Born on March 1, 1921, in New York City, the first of two sons of Lawrence Wilbur and Helen Purdy Wilbur, he moved to North Caldwell, New Jersey, when he was two. His father, a successful commercial artist who later became a portrait painter, and his mother, who came from a family of newspaper journalists, provided an idyllic if somewhat atypical childhood environment for their two sons. They rented a Colonial stone house on a four-hundred-and-fifty-acre "gentleman's farm" owned by a British textile manufacturer, Joshua Dickinson Armitage, who had taken a shine to Wilbur's father when meeting him on a golf course. The farm, Wilbur recalls, was staffed with a perfectly amiable mix of Armitage's relatives, other business associates, and employees. The farmhands were generous in their attentions to Wilbur and his younger brother Lawrence.

We were allowed to observe and interfere in all of their
operations – haying, silage-making, apple-picking, pig-
slaughter. . . . My childhood left me with a preference for
living in the sticks, for long walks, for physical work and
the raising of great crops of herbs and vegetables. . . .
It gave me an ability – essential in a poet – to make
something of solitude.[1]

In 1938 Wilbur entered Amherst College, where he majored
in English and edited the college newspaper. During two summers of his college years he hitchhiked and jumped freight
trains across America, a knockabout life that led the poet and
critic Dana Gioia to later quip, "Richard Wilbur may be the only
U.S. Poet Laureate to have been a hobo."

"Actually," Wilbur recalls,

I was a kind of privileged hobo. I kept a ten-dollar bill
in my boot and, in those days, bumming and hitching
your way across the country wasn't as perilous as it
might be now. I saw forty-six of the then forty-eight
states in this way; I saw all of the great cities, though I
observed them from the railroad yards out, a perspective I came to value.

During his Amherst years he fell in love with Charlotte Ward,
who was enrolled at nearby Smith College, Amherst's "sister
school." Wilbur remembers many occasions when he walked
the nine miles separating the two campuses to see "Charlee,"
and upon his graduation in 1942 they married.

World War II had already claimed some of Wilbur's class-
mates, and he enlisted soon after he married. Serving as a cryptographer with the U.S. Army, 36th Division, 36th Signal
Company, Wilbur saw almost immediate combat in the assault
on Monte Cassino, later at Anzio, and ultimately – by way of
southern France – at the Siegfried Line.

Our division took some heavy losses, but we signalmen, though often under fire, had fewer casualties than the line-company soldiers, of course. Our business was to maintain a web of communications connecting all commands within the division, and connecting the division to the army headquarters behind us. At one time or another I performed a number of functions – laying wire to the front, or operating a teletype, or carrying a message somewhere by jeep – but on the whole my occupation was to encipher and decipher radio messages. I enjoyed that work, because I have always been fond of puzzle solving. My small ability lay in solving enciphered messages which had been garbled in transmission; with my knowledge of Morse code, I was often able to guess what letters had been missent or misheard, and so go on deciphering a message to the end.

I wrote a number of war poems, but they were not like the poems full of the shock and horror that emerged from World War I – where a greater disillusionment permeated everything. In World War II we all felt that Hitler and his associates had to be resisted or we wouldn't have a world worth living in. And I, and thousands like me, came back to an applauding nation that wanted to give the veteran every possible break. Ours was not an experience like that of those poor devils, the veterans of Vietnam, who fought a fruitless war and came back to a public which largely scorned them.[2]

During the war Wilbur regularly wrote poems and sent some back to his wife. When she showed one to a friend who happened to be an editor at the *Saturday Evening Post*, the magazine published it immediately.

Wilbur chuckles about this almost effortless debut into publication.

I, like lots of soldiers at that time, was pouring my feelings into poems. Every daily issue of the *Stars and Stripes* had a column titled "Puptent Poets" – and if it's true that there are no atheists in foxholes, then let me tell you there were lots of poets in foxholes. When confronted with a world where chance seems to rule, articulateness is a great weapon. It was a good tonic for American soldiers to write poems. And even though I was imagining a career as a poet then, I'm pretty sure that the *Saturday Evening Post* might not have taken my poem except that it was by "Private Wilbur, one of our brave boys." It's true that I left the Army with $400 in my pocket, a wife and daughter to support, but I also returned to a country full of gratitude.

On the GI Bill Wilbur entered Harvard Graduate School, earning a masters degree in 1947. Subsequently, he was appointed a junior fellow, "that wonderful Harvard institution where they give you access to the facilities of the university and invite you to eat good lunches and good dinners in excellent company," he reports, his eyes twinkling. "I was writing poems at this time, but also I did a lot of work on Poe when I was a junior fellow, even trying to write a book about him. I'm still drawn to the symbolical or allegorical depth beneath Poe's prose and I'm continually discovering new things about him."

Like many Junior Fellows before him, Wilbur moved into the Harvard faculty in 1950 on a three-year appointment, joining the Cambridge world of writers and poets and scholars like F. O. Matthiessen and I. A. Richards, for whom he served as a teaching assistant; Robert Frost, who although nearly fifty years older, became a good friend.

Frost was actually very fond of my wife's family, as her grandfather, a literary editor, had been the first to publish his poems. He was also responsive to the fact that I knew many of his poems by heart. I loved the interplay between the conversational spontaneity and formal music of Frost's poems. And I was drawn to poems that offered, as his did, a rather simple surface meaning and a deeper text to be discovered. I could go back to my poems of Frost's and find something else, and then, something else.

"At that time I intended to be the best damned scholar of seventeenth-century culture there was – England, the Continent, arts, letters, I intended to do it all," he adds, but his skill as a poet and later as a translator and lyricist deflected him from his original path. While still in graduate school he published his first volume of poems, *The Beautiful Changes and Other Poems*, followed by *Ceremony and Other Poems* in 1950. *When Things of This World* (1956) won the Pulitzer Prize and the National Book Award, Wilbur's reputation as a poet was firmly established.

LOVE CALLS US TO THE THINGS OF THIS WORLD

The eyes open to a cry of pulleys,
And spirited from sleep, the astounded soul
Hangs for a moment bodiless and simple
As false dawn.
     Outside the open window
The morning air is all awash with angels.

Some are in bed-sheets, some are in blouses,
Some are in smocks: but truly there they are.
Now they are rising together in calm swells
Of halcyon feeling, filling whatever they wear
With the deep joy of their impersonal breathing;

Now they are flying in place, conveying
The terrible speed of their omnipresence, moving

And staying like white water; and now of a sudden
They swoon down into so rapt a quiet
That nobody seems to be there.
                              The soul shrinks

From all that it is about to remember,
From the punctual rape of every blessèd day,
And cries,
              "Oh, let there be nothing on earth but laundry,
Nothing but rosy hands in the rising steam
And clear dances done in the sight of heaven."

Yet, as the sun acknowledges
With a warm look the world's hunks and colors,
The soul descends once more in bitter love
To accept the waking body, saying now
In a changed voice as the man yawns and rises,

"Bring them down from their ruddy gallows;
Let there be clean linen for the backs of thieves;
Let lovers go fresh and sweet to be undone,
And the heaviest nuns walk in a pure floating
Of dark habits,
              keeping their difficult balance."

Wilbur's love of form, his ability to use rhyme, meter, and stanza to empower the arguments in his poems made his work immediately recognizable. The former cryptographer's love of the puzzle (and delight in solving it), the former seventeenth-century scholar's appreciation for intricate word play and competing arguments within the complementary envelope of the poem, the lover of Frost's surface-and-deep meanings all register in the unique figure a Wilbur poem makes.

Perhaps it's not surprising then that his poems seemed to invite critical analysis, the careful "close reading" techniques practiced by "the New Critics" in the fifties and sixties. The hand-and-glove fit of Wilbur's poems and the whole language of critical appreciation (*explication du texte*) that grew up around formalism proved as burdensome as it was laudatory. When formalism lost favor to the confessional school of poetry in the sixties and seventies and when a language of critical appreciation grew up around the confessional poets, Wilbur's work was sometimes challenged as "out of fashion": as intelligently conceived, but insufficiently ambitious, as distanced rather than immediate. "When those distinctions between 'palefaces' and 'redskins' came around, I was invariably 'a paleface' and when poetry was dubbed either 'raw' or 'cooked,' mine was definitely 'cooked.'" he observes wryly.[3] And although he paid a heavy price for refusing to "change," he prefers to take the long view when talking about poems and their accompanying critical schools of thought.

> I just kept doing what came naturally. The critical pendulum swung my way first, then away towards the confessionals, then back toward formalism. Despite the literary fashion, you have to be attuned to your own ear, your own gifts. The whole justification for form is that it helps to inform and orchestrate what is being said. A good poet is never one coerced by form, but a good poet needs to have turns, climaxes, joints – or he's left floundering in infinity. Robert Frost had a wonderful way of putting it. He said: "Bad poets rhyme words; good poets rhyme phrases." That's central to my way of composing a poem. I want the rhyme to happen inevitably, as a part of the flow of the argument – not as a way of completing an arbitrary pattern. That latter thing is just ornamentation: doily-making.[4]

Wilbur's friendship with Frost continued when he relocated to Wellesley to teach in 1953. And although "workshopping" poems with peers was not as popular in the early fifties as it would become later in the decade, Wilbur began to meet once a month with a group of poets that included John Holmes, John Ciardi, May Sarton, and Richard Eberhart. They met, more often than not, in John Holmes's Medford home, each bringing a new poem for reading and discussion – a format very similar to the Holmes-led workshop attended a few years later by Maxine Kumin and Anne Sexton. He also befriended several slightly younger poets like Philip Booth (who was also teaching at Wellesley) and Donald Hall (before he left the Boston area for Ann Arbor). Hall, in fact, recalls with amusement a day he and Wilbur spent at Suffolk Downs, a nearby race track. Wilbur chose to bet on horses that were beautiful, while Hall studied his Racing Form, carefully calculating the odds before placing his bets. He remembers at the end of the day they came out about forty cents apart. Wilbur also met the poet Sylvia Plath and wrote a poem about that occasion that generated a hot controversy.

Cottage Street, 1953

Framed in her phoenix fire-screen, Edna Ward
Bends to the tray of Canton, pouring tea
For frightened Mrs. Plath; then, turning toward
The pale, slumped daughter, and my wife, and me,

Asks if we would prefer it weak or strong.
Will we have milk or lemon, she enquires?
The visit seems already strained and long.
Each in his turn, we tell her our desires.

It is my office to exemplify
The published poet in his happiness,
Thus cheering Sylvia, who has wished to die;
But half-ashamed, and impotent to bless,

I am a stupid life-guard who has found,
Swept to his shallows by the tide, a girl
Who, far from shore, has been immensely drowned,
And stares through water now with eyes of pearl.

How large is her refusal; and how slight
The genteel chat whereby we recommend
Life, of a summer afternoon, despite
The brewing dusk which hints that it may end.

And Edna Ward shall die in fifteen years,
After her eight-and-eighty summers of
Such grace and courage as permit no tears,
The thin hand reaching out, the last word love,

Outliving Sylvia who, condemned to live,
Shall study for a decade, as she must,
To state at last her brilliant negative
In poems free and helpless and unjust.

"'Cottage Street, 1953' is almost the sole poem of mine that could be classified as "confessional." It simply tells what happened. Prior to the occasion of that poem, if I remember rightly, I had met Sylvia Plath just once, when she was working for *Mademoiselle* and did some interviews with four young teachers of writing, myself and Tony Hecht among them. 'Cottage Street' takes place in Wellesley, at my mother-in-law's house, soon after Sylvia Plath had attempted to take her own life. Mrs. Plath and Mrs. Ward evidently felt that it would do Sylvia good to have tea with someone who represented a cheerful version of the poet's life. I was aware of that and found it a tough assignment."

I interject quickly, "That was a brave poem, and probably one you took a lot of heat for."

"So I did. The critics of Plath's poems were from the first

contentious and proprietary, and I was accused by some of anti-confessionalism, or professional envy, or anti-feminism, or shallowness. That concluding word, 'unjust,' must have seemed to some like the sting of a scorpion. Later, in 1995 or so, I was pleased to get a letter from Ted Hughes which said that my poem was 'the truest, best thing' to have been written about Sylvia Plath."

"Some probably wouldn't find him an impartial judge," I add.

"That's so, but his letter compensated for some of the negative criticism I'd taken. I think most people see now that I was trying, in that poem, to be fair to everybody concerned, and sympathetic too – trying to present, as honestly as possible, a contrast between Edna Ward and her young guest."

In addition to writing and publishing poems steadily, Wilbur began to explore another form of creative expression – verse drama. Following the war, verse drama had enjoyed a revival, fueled by the work of T. S. Eliot and Christopher Fry in England and Archibald MacLeish in the United States. A new drama company called the Poets' Theater in Cambridge, Massachusetts, had begun to stage original verse plays and foreign classics in contemporary translations. Wilbur won a Guggenheim Fellowship and set out to New Mexico for a year to try his hand at writing verse drama.

> I sat in an adobe house in Corrales and wrote and wrote and wrote. The results were, shall we say, arid. While I could write the dialogue, I could not create real characters, and the results were extremely wooden. I decided that I might learn the craft by translating Molière's classic comedy, The Misanthrope.

This experiment in creating a rhymed English version of a comedy by a seventeenth-century French dramatist began what many critics have characterized as one of the greatest literary translations projects in American literature. Over the next forty years Wilbur would create witty, sophisticated, and highly dramatic versions of many of Molière's comedies, as well as two neo-classical verse tragedies by Racine. Wilbur's versions have played to enthusiastic audiences from Broadway to tiny college campus black box theaters, creating something of a revival of Molière.

With the success of *The Misanthrope*, Wilbur was contacted by composer Leonard Bernstein and playwright Lillian Hellman to write the lyrics for a musical comedy based on Voltaire's *Candide*, a project they had been struggling to complete for almost five years. The enterprise was challenging.

Wilbur remembers:

Bernstein and Hellman were much heavier hitters than I. Each was accustomed to running the show and, of course, a poet is accustomed to doing what he does without interference. I'd have to characterize Lillian as warm and affectionate most of the time. We didn't have any major fallings-out. Admittedly, Lenny and I had our moments – probably all the predictable troubles between a composer and a lyricist. But almost immediately I enjoyed the work and discovered I had some talent for it.

When I was an adolescent and into my college days I played the guitar. Mostly I sang folk songs and the blues. It wasn't very artful, but if you sing poorly and you play poorly, the two can come together in a rather touching way. So I already had some pleasant experiences matching words to music. As I worked at it, I discovered that writing witty lyrics with just the right kind of texture was my strength.

We did have some wonderful moments in *Candide*. Tony Guthrie, our director, would suddenly stop the show, yelling, "That won't do." "Wilbur, go into the men's room and come out in ten minutes with some new material." One night in Boston, Lenny and I decided that a certain spot in the show was going dead. We needed a rousing number – one right on the verge of vulgarity. So we sat up the whole night and wrote a new number; it was in rehearsal the next afternoon.

That piece, "What's the Use?" now ranks among the classics in American musical theater.

In addition to the translations of plays, each of Wilbur's volumes of poems since *Ceremony* has included verse translations, usually derived from French or Italian poets, but also including poems from Russian, Portuguese, Spanish, and Hungarian authors. "Although I try to catch, in so far as I can, the technical requirements of sonnets, or ballades, it is the emotional content that is the challenge when translating. Fidelity to the spirit of the piece is much more important than fidelity to the word."

Teaching has also been central to his working life. After his three-year stint at Wellesley, he received an appointment at Wesleyan University in Connecticut where he not only taught for twenty years, but also initiated the Wesleyan University Press's poetry program, whose success led other university presses to establish poetry lists of their own.

If the task of reading more than one hundred poetry manuscripts during any given year proved onerous, Wilbur was also positioned to help deserving manuscripts find their way into publication. One such fortuitous opportunity came when in 1957 he ran into Stanley Kunitz at a party in New York. Wilbur had read Kunitz's work for years and respected it highly; he was appalled when he discovered that after thirty years of publishing poetry of the highest caliber, Kunitz now found himself without a publisher. Wilbur asked to read the new poems, then wrote to his old friend Emily Morison Beck at Atlantic Monthly Press, recommending that she publish a *Selected Poems* by

Kunitz. He advised, it will be "one of the best poetry manu-scripts of the century." He also predicted it would win the Pulitzer Prize.[5]

Following an almost twenty-year tenure at Wesleyan, the Wilburs moved back to the communities of their college years – Amherst and Northampton, Massachusetts, and where Wilbur taught for the next decade, until retirement, at Smith College.

> I was an over-preparer for my classes, sometimes aver-aging as much as six or seven hours of preparation time for one hour of classroom time. I was fortunate in often having literature courses to teach, where I could reread the classics and refresh my memory of the enduring texts. I enjoyed teaching writing courses less, I think, and perhaps that's why I always began courses on the writing of poems with two long lectures on prosody. That's so deadly dull that I knew I'd retain only those who were serious about writing.

A recent poem, published in the *New Yorker*, suggests that Wilbur has continued to keep good counsel with Robert Frost, delighting in the specific details of a New England landscape while still planting meanings as deep as a reader cares to dig.

BLACKBERRIES FOR AMELIA

Fringing the woods, the stone walls, and the lanes,
Old thickets everywhere have come alive,
Their new leaves reaching out in fans of five
From tangles overarched by this year's canes.

They have their flowers too, it being June,
And here or there in brambled dark-and-light
Are small, five-petaled blooms of chalky white,
As random-clustered and as loosely strewn

As the far stars, of which we now are told
That ever faster do they bolt away,
And that a night may come in which, some say,
We shall have only blackness to behold.

I have no time for any change so great,
But I shall see the August weather spur
berries to ripen where the flowers were –
Dark berries, savage-sweet and worth the wait –

And there will come the moment to be quick
And save some from the birds, and I shall need
Two pails, old clothes in which to stain and bleed,
And a grandchild to talk with while we pick.

I don't suppose it's surprising that the solitary life, the world a little apart from the city or the college, has always been my dwelling place. Charlee and I have always been country people. When we needed to be at Harvard, we lived in Lincoln; when we needed to be at Wesleyan, we lived across the river in Portland; when I began to teach at Smith College, we were already in the process of restoring this place in the country. I like to be in touch with the seasons, to work in my garden, to move with the natural rhythms of things.[6]

Equipoise, grace, affirmation are not always anticipated in poets, who have frequently been portrayed in popular culture as angst ridden and self-destructive. Richard Wilbur has, at times, stood in sharp relief from the dominant tones of his literary age: he has been cheerful in the Age of Anxiety, he has been a formalist in an age of restless experimentation, and he has been Apollonian in temperament in an age of Dionysian spillage. Further, he excels in literary forms that some contemporary critics have undervalued: verse translations, Broadway lyrics, poems that read like religious or classical allegories, comic verse that turns on puns or paradoxes.

His has been a "difficult balance" – to refuse to be silenced, to continue to be true to his instincts and creative gifts, to survive (to use images from his beloved Poe) the swinging of the critical Pendulum without being either eviscerated or pushed into its engulfing Pit. He has written and sailed on the keel of his own fashioning. In 1989, his *New and Collected Poems* earned a second Pulitzer Prize, rendering him the only living American poet to have won that award twice.

Several years ago, when questioned by his good friend and fellow writer, Paul Mariani, about the religious subtext in many of his poems, a sacramental vision that envisions the world as shimmering with possibility, Wilbur explained: "What doesn't particularly interest me in religion is the Creed. The Creed strikes me as some sort of political platform, and indeed, that's probably what it was. What I respond to is *Lift up your hearts!*"[7]

ENDNOTES

1. Peter Dale, *Richard Wilbur* (London: Between the Lines Publishers, 2000), 17–18. This is one of the most wide-ranging interviews with Richard Wilbur, of interest to general readers and specialists alike. On pages 17–18 and 20–24, Wilbur discusses at some length his experiences criss-crossing the county as a hobo and serving in the signal company in World War II.

2. Ibid.

3. Wilbur has spoken about academic schools of criticism in many interviews, particularly in *Conversations with Richard Wilbur*, William Butts, ed., (Jackson, Mississippi and London: University of Mississippi Press, 1990); Peter Dale's interview mentioned in the previous citation, Peter Davison, *The Fading Smile: Poets in Boston from Robert Frost to Robert Lowell to Sylvia Plath,*

1955–1960, (New York: Knopf, 1994), and Peter Stitt, *The World's Hieroglyphic Beauty: Five American Poets*, (Athens, The University of Georgia Press, 1985).

4. As poetry editor of the *Atlantic Monthly*, Peter Davison interviewed Wilbur in 1999 for *Atlantic Unbound*, focusing particularly on his use of form. Wilbur had this to say:

> Every form I think has a certain logic, has certain expressive capa-
> bilities. Most of the time the ideas that come to us have no business
> being thrust into, say, the sonnet form. If we did that, the form
> would be making demands, would be directing the show. But if one
> chooses form rightly, one is not submitting to the demands of the
> form, but using form to enhance the argument.

5. Davison, *The Fading Smile*, 75.

6. *In The Fading Smile*, p. 68, Davison suggests that the Wilbur' desire to locate in the country stemmed both from their realization that "we are country folks" and from Wilbur's desire to keep his poetic life and his academic life separate, even at some geographical remove, one from the other.

7. Paul Mariani, "A Conversation with Richard Wilbur," *Image*, no. 12 (Winter 95–96).

Maxine Kumin

THAT INNER COMPASS

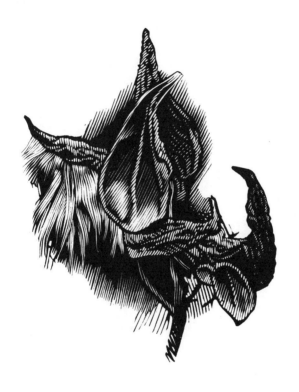

Maxine Kumin

T HE LAST COUPLE OF MILES of back-country corduroy road somewhere outside of Warner, New Hampshire (population 2,500), requires a certain strength of spine and axle. Climbing steadily uphill on a deeply rutted dirt road, a visitor can't miss the hand-lettered sign posted high on a spreading maple: PoBiz Farm. It announces, unmistakably, the home of Maxine Kumin. Around one remaining tricky curve and the vista of the farm opens: to the right, a classic two-hundred-year-old twin-chimneyed farmhouse, freshly painted dark red, its front porch enclosed and its south-facing wooden deck and terrace overlooking a small fire pond (the nearest fire hydrant is several miles away); to the left, a weathered barn stacked on the steep incline of the hill, with horse stalls constructed on the lower level, out of the stinging winds and frigid air of a New England winter. Heavily forested and granite strewn, the farm reveals itself in increments, progressive clearings, each notched into slopes too steep for machinery to navigate. Perhaps fifty yards uphill a broader plateau opens, accommodating a flourishing vegetable garden and a large pond for swimming. Beyond the pond, on the property's "only truly level piece of earth" is a dressage and riding ring constructed by Maxine and her husband Victor, who not only installed all the fencing, but also picked the stones out by hand and smoothed the surface to an even plane. Even higher is "The Elysian Field," the highest pasture on the property, with a commanding view of the surrounding Mink Hills.

The Kumins have fenced fourteen acres of forage fields for

their animals, acreage they must lime, fertilize, and mow. This upland farm, a two-hundred-acre spread (most of which is now in conservation), is both the subject and inspiration for many of Maxine Kumin's poems, memoirs, and essays. Foraging for wild mushrooms, feeding the animals, mulching the garden, mowing the grass provide "meditative time" when, she suggests, "my hands are busy, but my mind is busier." As she observes in the essay collection about life on the farm, *In Deep*, "Location is where we start from. Landscape provides our first geography, the turn of the seasons our archetypes for our own mortality."[1]

Slender, athletic, with chiselled features and a thick mane of salt and pepper hair, Maxine Kumin moves with the careful calculation of someone who has had to regain equilibrium, relearn the motor skills necessary to walk on hilly terrain and open the multiple latches of fence gates and stall doors on the farm. In fact, in 1998 she suffered a near-fatal accident while participating in a horse-driving clinic – practicing a sport in which she and her chestnut horse Deuter were well schooled and highly competitive. Spooked first by a runaway horse and then by a noisy logging truck that clanged by, Deuter bolted, ejecting Kumin from the 350-pound driving rig. In his efforts to avoid stepping on her, the horse dragged the rig over her prone body. The result was devastating: a "hangman's fracture" of the neck, eleven broken ribs, a punctured lung, a bruised kidney and liver, and massive internal bleeding. Kumin was forced to spend months and months of rehabilitation inside an axial traction head-immobilizing device called a "halo." After a period of partial paralysis, of being "treated like a marionette" – her arms and legs moved by others – she worked to regain full use of her arms, legs, and hands; to relearn the tricky art of balance when walking an "uphill farm" and negotiating the floors of the vintage farmhouse where some of the wide pine planks have settled at uneven angles.

"Ninety-five percent of people with your fracture never

make it to the emergency room," her doctor confided later, "and 95 percent of the ones who do, end up as quadriplegics." Kumin has not only survived, she has – to borrow Faulkner's famous word – "prevailed," writing a memoir about the accident and its aftermath, *Inside the Halo and Beyond*; a volume of essays, *Always Beginning*; a mystery novel, *Quit Monks or Die*; and two volumes of poems, *The Long Marriage* and *Jack, and Other New Poems*. If she walks with necessary caution, there's nothing tentative about the way she faces life, nor the way she writes about her discoveries.

"Clearly, the impulse for poems exists here for me, in the vivid turn of the seasons, in the dailiness of growing things, in the quite primitive satisfaction of putting up vegetables and fruits, gathering wild nuts and mushrooms, raising meat for the table, collecting sap for sweetening," she writes in *In Deep*.[2] "And there's a kind of camaraderie of other halfway-hill people. You'd be surprised how many of us there are, hidden in the pleats and folds of the hills."[3]

The farm was a gift, in a way, and also the product of a search. Kumin has told the story of its acquisition often, but repetition hasn't dulled her delight in the details.

In 1963 both Victor and I inherited $5,000. Mine came from my grandmother's estate and it was Victor's mother who died, leaving him that legacy. Ten thousand dollars was a lot of money in 1963.

We were living in Newton, a suburb of Boston, the kids were all in the public schools there, and we had been talking about finding a weekend place – one close enough to Boston to allow for an easy commute to Victor's engineering job. We had honeymooned not too far from this place on a farm up in East Andover. We made friends with the farmer and his wife, had visited with them over the years, and they put us on to a realtor who showed us three places in the area. This was the third place; as soon as we started up the hill I got goosebumps – I knew this was *the place*.

It had stood empty for at least six years, and it was in deplorable shape. Although the twin-chimney Colonial farmhouse captivated us, it was in disrepair, listing to one side on rotted sills. It had no insulation or storm windows, and no heat except woodstoves. Electricity was in, as well as a pure spring-fed well and fairly functional plumbing, but the "lawn" was also so overgrown with sumac and blackberry that we had to hack away to even look in the windows.

The barn looked even worse. Although forty dairy cows were once sheltered there, the whole back end of it wobbled and if you looked up through the haymow you could see the sky. But at that point we only intended to use the farm as a getaway place – holidays, weekends, and we really didn't intend to pour a whole lot of money into it. The sellers were anxious to move it, an artist and his wife who had divorced and would let us have the entire property for $11,000. That was a little over our budget, but we bought it outright. We had the protection of innocence.

Victor is a practical engineer, one who can figure things out, disassemble, reassemble, fix many things. He invited a few of his colleagues up for a Sunday picnic and they trooped around, doing a thorough examination of the house, barn, and adjoining fields and woods. In their explorations they discovered a marshy area above the house that could make a good pond, and with the help of the Federal Soil Conservation Service, we dug a two-thirds-of-an-acre pond that first summer of 1963.

Gradually we set about restoring the place – hard, if rewarding labor that's lasted for forty years now. The first friends we made had an equine farm across town – nothing fancy, just a grassroots place where our middle daughter, Judith, went to learn to ride. She went absolutely wild over horses and I guess, in the process, I got infected too. We started out by taking two leased horses. Then we took on two newly weaned foals. Ultimately, we bought a horse, then rescued another – and for the first twelve years we'd stable the horses on the property during the summers and board them out from Labor Day to June first.

Then I started to garden. [A mischievous smile plays at the corners of her mouth.] And of course I felt I *had* to come up from Boston early to get my seedlings in – mulching them with *New York Times Book Review* cutworm collars; then I *had* to stay late in order to harvest everything and put up jams, jellies, applesauce, beans, peas, beets.

When we bought the place the children were at easy ages: Jane, twelve and one-half, Judith, eleven, and Danny, eight. As they moved into their teen years, I noticed that many of their friends were beginning to think of the farm as a focus for their social life. Whole carloads of them would arrive over the weekends, exploring the trails and fields, sometimes digging postholes or tacking up shingles in the afternoons, and spreading out their ten or twelve sleeping bags on the living room floor at night. It was clear that we were all becoming more and more attached to the place.

By 1976 we were ready to become year-rounders. Victor continued to work as a consulting engineer, commuting to Boston twice a week, and I centered my life here, writing and caring for the farm and the horse business we'd begun. (We began to cross-breed Arabians with Standardbreds, the trotters of harness-racing fame, when we became interested in the sport of distance riding.) I continued to schedule poetry readings and workshops, traveling all over the United States, the "PoBiz"

that accounts for much of my livelihood – and that pays
most of the horse bills."[4]

In the past, the Kumins stuffed the barn with horses, sheep, and
goats, but now they keep only two horses: the legendary,
"bombproof" Boomer, now twenty-seven, and Deuter, a gor-
geous, red chestnut gelding who carries the size and strength of
his Standardbred mother. Despite the terrible accident, Kumin
steadfastly refuses to place blame on "the Dude," as she calls
him affectionately, and when she whistles for him to come, he
roars in from the back pasture, his eyes full of trust and delight.
Two rescued dogs are family members: Virgil, a short-haired,
muscular mostly-hound type, has full run of the property, while
Xochi, a white, wooly mop of a guy, formerly a Mexican street
dog, reigns supreme inside the house. Kumin volunteers, "His
immigration papers read 'macho mestizo'" – perhaps loosely
translated as "mutt with an attitude" – and Xochi appears to
have read them. Wendy, a riding companion of Maxine's and
an "excellent horse person," comes in a couple afternoons a
week to help with the garden and horses, and Roger, a live-in
custodian, serves as a back up for Victor. At work on a new children's book, Kumin is also teaching this year at New England
College – just twenty minutes down the road. Invitations to
give readings and participate in panel discussions on the literary
arts arrive with regularity. "When I leave the farm it's strictly for
business. I do travel a fair amount, though my kids used to joke
that it was hard to get me past the mailbox – unless I was on
horseback," she admits, laughingly.

Kumin has always enjoyed physical activity. A self-pro-
claimed "jock" all her life, she was a competitive swimmer in
her college days and continues to swim daily in the pond as long
as weather permits; when temperatures drop too low for comfort, she switches to the Olympic-size pool in nearby New London. Yet it is not simply staying physically active that motivates

her. She believes there is "a zen" in swimming, gardening, mowing: that the muse and physical activity are connected.

MORNING SWIM

Into my empty head there come
a cotton beach, a dock wherefrom

I set out, oily and nude
through mist, in chilly solitude.

There was no line, nor roof or floor
to tell the water from the air.

Night fog thick as terry cloth
closed me in its fuzzy growth.

I hung my bathrobe on two pegs.
I took the lake between my legs.

Invaded and invader, I
went overhand on that flat sky.

Fish twitched beneath me, quick and tame,
In their green zone they sang my name.

And in the rhythm of the swim
I hummed a two-four-time slow hymn.

I hummed Abide with Me. *The beat*
rose in the fine thrash of my feet,

rose in the bubbles I put out
slantwise, trailing through my mouth.

My bones drank water; water fell
through all my doors. I was the well

that fed the lake that met my sea
in which I sang Abide with Me.

Sound is of particular importance in my poems. And I
know I write better poems in form – with the demands
of a rhyme scheme and a metrical pattern – than I do in
the looser line of free verse. Without form I'd feel like
I was abandoned in flat Indiana with my eyelids sewn
open.

When she teaches courses in poetry she recommends that her
students commit to memory whole poems and significant
numbers of stanzas from long, narrative poems, amassing a
"memory bank" in case they "are seized as political prisoners."

"There's something deeply gratifying about incantatory
sounds," she says, adding that when she was subject to the "terrible rapping" of MRIs, she sought comfort in repeating poems
from memory. Like the Vietnam POWs who survived incarcer-
ation in the "Hanoi Hilton" by tapping out words on cell walls
that they later constructed into fragments of remembered
poems, Kumin believes we can all benefit from collecting an
"inner library."

Born in Germantown, a residential section of northwest
Philadelphia, in 1925, Kumin grew up with three older brothers on the edge of Fairmount Park, a sprawling park complex
that runs from the center of the city out into the suburbs.
Before the age of anxiety over child abductions and muggings,
she and her cousins enjoyed enormous freedoms in the park,
often spending all day in the woods, or – as she remembers
vividly – lying in wait for a mounted park guard to come by
who might just permit her to sit on his horse.

Although the Kumins were Jewish, Maxine attended a convent school run by the teaching order, the Sisters of St. Joseph. It was largely a matter of convenience since the school was next door and the public school, before the days of busing, was more than a mile away. The family had a Christmas tree and also celebrated Hanukkah. "We really had everything an uneasy assimilation in suburbia allows," she recalls, while admitting that she grew up in an era when anti-Semitism was still overt.[5]

Summers found her at Camp Watitoh in the Berkshires where she perfected her swimming skills, dreaming of a berth on the women's Olympic swim team. In fact, she was attracted to Wellesley College primarily because it had an Olympic-size swimming pool, but the admissions committee didn't look favorably on her candidacy, and she went to Radcliffe as a history and literature major in 1942.

Most of America's young men were going off to war, including all three of Maxine's brothers. Through mutual friends she met Victor Kumin, a recent Harvard graduate, now a staff sergeant in the army, who was home on a brief furlough. Their courtship was intense, partly conducted via "a marathon of letter writing." Just after her graduation from Radcliffe in 1946 and three weeks after Victor was mustered out of the army, they married. It was, and is a "marriage for life," as Victor likes to say.

She completed a master's degree in comparative literature at Harvard, though "hugely pregnant" with their first child, Jane. Eighteen months later Judith was born and three years after that Danny came along. In 1957, with three children under the age of ten, Kumin signed up for a poetry workshop conducted by poet and Tufts University professor John Holmes at the Boston Center for Adult Education. It was a move that would change her life, since not only did she begin to write seriously under Holmes's tutelage, but it was there that she met Anne Sexton, also a young wife and mother, a former fashion model, whose enormous talent was balanced precariously on the edge of mental breakdowns and depressions and who had come to poetry at the suggestion of her therapist. Finding in one another some magnetic essence, they would remain best friends and ideal readers of one another's work for almost eighteen years.

Prompted by Holmes to join the New England Poetry Club, a literary organization that was composed at that time "mostly of Boston Brahmins of a certain age," Kumin and Sexton found themselves admitted at first reluctantly to the inner sanctum. Kumin remembers that initially members of the club had difficulty telling them apart: after all, they were both young mothers from the suburbs, tall, slender, with dark hair. Sexton had an even more brash interpretation: "You know why they can't tell us apart? They can't figure out who's the Jew and who's the kook."[6]

Introductions to other writers by Holmes, membership in the Poetry Club, and the steady publication of poems in magazines like the *New Yorker* and *Harper's* resulted in multiple readings and a steady, cumulative recognition. In 1961, Kumin and Sexton were selected for chapter membership in the Radcliffe Institute for Independent Study, later renamed the Bunting Institute (currently, and ironically, reborn as the Radcliffe Institute for Independent Study, now admitting men). Here they enjoyed weekly seminars with gifted women working in a whole variety of fields. Painters, historians, social scientists, and sculptors joined with writers to present papers, to discuss work, to share the same space and, to a large extent, the same mission.

It's hard to overestimate the perspective conferred by that year at the Bunting. When Anne and I first began publishing, women poets were frequently dismissed as "immature" or given over to "hysteria," or capable of writing only "domestic" poems. To be in the company of that many talented, serious-minded and ambitious women, each pursuing excellence in her chosen field, was affirming in ways we really hadn't experienced before. We found a legitimacy and a recognition that came all too rarely to women writers.

Their friendship was also affirming. "We were able to cheer each other on. . . . I can't say I was never jealous of her stellar rise to fame. But if becoming a contract writer for the *New Yorker* couldn't happen to me, I reasoned, having it happen to Annie was the next best outcome."[7]

But Sexton's mental state, fragile at best, "rose and fell like a fever chart." Always flamboyant and glamorous, famous for creating an air "of emotional turbulence" when she took to the stage, outfitted in her signature blood-red dress to read her poems in front of sold-out audiences, Sexton was becoming famous. Her career "took off like a rocket," while Maxine Kumin's climbed steadily, if more slowly. If Sexton benefited from the stabilizing influence of Kumin in her life and work, then Kumin opened to new freedoms and risks in her work "because of Annie." They "workshopped" their own works in progress by keeping a phone line open between their houses when working on poems. When one needed the attention of the other, she would whistle into the receiver and then proceed to ask for advice.

Alcohol, a bewildering array of antipsychotic drugs, and a succession of ill-fated love affairs took Sexton closer and closer to the edge. Most of her intimate friends admitted to one another that, eventually, she would die by her own hand. Their final lunch together in the Kumin home in Newton, however, betrayed no clues of her intention. They went over the galleys of Sexton's about-to-be-published poetry collection, *An Awful Rowing Toward God*, ate tuna fish sandwiches (and Anne had two double vodkas), walked together out to the car, hugged and parted. Less than four hours later, Sexton let herself into her garage, arranged herself in the driver's seat of her Cougar, then turned on the ignition.

How It Is

Shall I say how it is in your clothes?
A month after your death I wear your blue jacket.
The dog at the center of my life recognizes
you've come to visit, he's ecstatic.

In the left pocket, a hole.
In the right, a parking ticket
delivered up last August on Bay State Road.
In my heart, a scatter like milkweed,
a flinging from the pods of the soul.
My skin presses your old outline.
It is hot and dry inside.

I think of the last day of your life,
old friend, how I would unwind it, paste
it together in a different collage,
back from the death car idling in the garage,
back up the stairs, your praying hands unlaced,
reassembling the bites of bread and tuna fish
into a ceremony of sandwich,
running the home movie backward to a space
we could be easy in, a kitchen place,
with vodka and ice, our words like living meat.

Dear friend, you have excited crowds
with your example. They swell
like wine bags, straining at your seams.
I will be years gathering up our words,
fishing out letters, snapshots, stains,
leaning my ribs against this durable cloth,
to put on the dumb blue blazer of your death.

Anne Sexton's suicide, just eleven years after poet Sylvia Plath
died by her own hand, ignited a firestorm – literary, psycholog-

ical, social, and cultural – reassessing the "confessional school of poetry": poets like Robert Lowell, W. D. Snodgrass, John Berryman, and Anne Sexton who excavated in their poems the pain and turmoil of their own lives. Women poets were especially subject to scrutiny, stretched as they were between the forces that continued to threaten or censor full self-expression and the urgency to break free of those inhibitors. By the late 1970s the feminist movement was identifying, in Adrienne Rich's words, "the murderous consequences of believing the images the patriarchy has held up to us."[8] To recognize the script of the oppressor without internalizing its messages, to, in fact, subvert the tradition into which one is born became the mandate of the feminist movement. Plath and Sexton were enshrined within that movement, as was Kumin, who continues to wear the label "feminist" as a badge of honor, even if she confesses some surprise at "seeing my name in all the history books." Referred to as one who helped revise the content of poetry – enlarging it to include a "previously inadmissable constellation of feelings,"[9] or as Carolyn Kizer famously phrased it, "merely the private lives of one-half of humanity" – Kumin acknowledges that poetry's subject matter and scope have altered in the course of her lifetime. Plath's poems, Sexton's poems, Rich's poems, and Kumin's poems have helped effect that change.

If Sexton and Kumin imagined, jokingly, growing into old age together, walking down Fifth Avenue in custom-made shoes, Dalmatians heeling by their sides:

> Bad girls of the New England Poetry Club
> our wit and fame up ahead
> leading a procession of disciples.[10]

they were, at least metaphorically, not far wrong.

* * *

Maxine Kumin's literary output is prodigious. In addition to fif-teen volumes of poems, five novels, a collection of short sto-ries, a memoir, and four collections of essays, she has published more than twenty children's books. If she is skilled in a variety of genres, she considers herself, first and foremost, a poet, declaring: "If the Muse came down and said choose, I'd have to say poetry." And in 1973 her excellence as a poet was rewarded nationally: *Up Country: Poems of New England* won the Pulitzer Prize. Volumes of poems have followed in regular two-to-three year intervals ever since.

In fact, Kumin's reputation as a poet resulted in her appoint-ment as Consultant to the Library of Congress (a position now titled Poet Laureate); she used her year in Washington to pro-vide outreach for teachers, primarily in public high schools.

I wanted to try to break down the standard approach to teaching poetry, which was then and I'm afraid still may be, killing a poem with creeping exegesis: explain-ing away a poem's possibilities, looking for the "right answer" to a poem's meaning. I had a very good time instituting once a week brown bag lunches in the Library's august poetry room and I invited various writ-ers in to talk about their work. We made it a kind of neighborhood thing, each person also invited to bring along a disciple; we'd all sit together on the oriental rug.

I suppose some of my conscious interest in outreach work stems from the fact that women role models really didn't exist for me. Marianne Moore was too quirky. Elizabeth Bishop was too detached, too classical. When I was sixteen I committed lots of Edna St. Vincent Mil-lay's sonnets to heart, but they didn't have the intellec-tual bite or attraction I felt in, say, Yeats or Auden. Perhaps if I had known Louise Bogan's work or Muriel Rukeyser's poems I would have gravitated toward them. But they really didn't come to light until later.

I've lived long enough to see patterns of mentoring emerge: male poets mentoring younger male poets and women poets and writers providing support and encouragement for other women writers. Cross-fertilization is more rare. Actually, I have seen a few marvelous crossovers: Tony Hecht, for example, immediately loved Alicia Ostriker's poems and said so in print. And Stanley Kunitz has championed young women poets for several generations – from Maxine Kumin to Louise Glück, to Marie Howe. He has been a bulwark.[11]

By her own assertion, Kumin's poetry has grown more political over the years – "bolder, certainly darker" in the last two decades.[12] Some suggest that the political issues and hard-edged explorations of some recent poems are occasioned by conversations with her daughter Judith, who was with the United Nations High Commissioner for Refugees, a job that pulled her to the hot spots of the world – Belgrade, Bangkok – where she dealt with groups like the Vietnamese boat people, the displaced and disenfranchised of the world.

Yes, I am very close to Judith. She was simply invaluable to us, coming home after I had the accident and helping in my recovery in all the ways that matter. We have always had hard discussions about children and animals who are abandoned, seemingly forgotten when civil conflicts, national wars, invasions of various kinds wreak their havoc. But it's not simply Judith's work that is taking me this direction. We're all, poets included, dealing with global issues of survival, of genocide, of hunger. We can see the torture and the killings and the barbarism on TV each night, in color, in our living rooms. How does a poet write poems in the face of this reality? And what can we hope to accomplish?

I don't think poets speak with one voice about this

dilemma. In fact, the only time we stand up in united protest is when Laura Bush invites us to the White House. But I do know that, for me, these are poems I must write for sanity's sake and because it is important to bear witness. Surely a poet's role in the culture is to run ahead in the darkness and hold up a vision of what is true.[13]

WANT

The world is awash in unwanted dogs;
like-alike yellow curly-haired mongrels that come
collared and wormed, neutered and named, through customs
come immunized, racketing and rabies-tagged

to Midwestern farms from Save the Children, the Peace Corps
come from Oxfam into the carpeted bedrooms of embassies
into the Brooklyn lofts of CARE workers on leave
into the London, Paris, Geneva homes of Doctors Without Borders

and still the streets of Asmara, Kigali, Bombay
refill with ur-dogs: those bred-back scavenging flea-ridden
sprung-ribbed bitches whose empty teats make known
the latest bitten-off litter of curs that go back to the Pleistocene.

And what of the big-headed stick-figured children naked
in the doorways of Goma, Luanda, Juba, Les Hants
or crouched in the dust of the haphazard donkey-width tracks
that connect the named and the nameless hamlets of Want?

There will always be those who speed past unbeguiled.
There will always be somewhere a quorum of holy fools
who wade into the roiling sea despite the tsunami
to dip teaspoon after teaspoon from the ocean.

Whatever the world situation, whatever the poet's role,
I think it is almost impossible to identify what steers my
poems: probably an inner compass that I'm not even
conscious of. I see the direction a poem will take only as
it's taking it. My job is to be open, attentive. I love that
line from Rilke, "Await the birth-hour of a new clarity,
keeping holy all that befalls, even disappointment, even
desertion." I try to keep that in my mind, even when
"keeping holy all that befalls" is difficult.[14]

Descending the steep driveway is less grueling than climbing it
and in the rearview mirror the full vista of the farm appears,
each of its cleared levels now alive with function and possibility. Kumin is coming out onto the terrace to gather cherry
tomatoes, basil, and leaf lettuce from one of the large wooden
containers that line the ridge; Xochi, a white exclamation point
at her feet. She lifts her hand in a gesture, half salute, half
farewell; after all, it's feeding time.

ENDNOTES

1. Maxine Kumin, "A Sense of Place," in *In Deep: Country Essays* (New York: Viking, 1987), 170.

2. Kumin, *In Deep*, 162.

3. Ibid., 8.

4. Maxine Kumin has written extensively about the acquisition of PoBiz Farm, the stewardship of the land, and the care and love of animals. See *In Deep, To Make a Prairie: Essays on Poets, Poetry, and Country Living* (1980), and *Women, Animals, & Vegetables: Essays and Stories* (1994).

5. Kumin speaks more about her Jewish heritage, its presence in her life and work, in "For Anne at Passover," *Always Beginning* (2000).

6. Diane Wood Middlebrook's biography, *Anne Sexton*, (Boston: Houghton Mifflin, 1991). This work provides a richly detailed account of Sexton's troubled and brilliant life and discusses at length her close friendship with Maxine Kumin. See also Diana Hume George, *Oedipus Anne: The Poetry of Anne Sexton* (Urbana and Chicago: University of Illinois Press, 1987), and Alicia Ostriker, *Stealing the Language: The Emergence of Women's Poetry in America.* (Boston: Beacon Press, 1986).

7. Numerous Kumin poems have Anne Sexton as their emotional center; additionally, Kumin has explored their friendship in several essays: "October 4, 1995," "For Anne at Passover," and "Motherhood and Politics" are in *Always Beginning.* Also see Kumin, "How It Was," in *Sexton: Selected Criticism*, Diana Hume George, ed. (Urbana and Chicago: University of Illinois Press, 1988).

8. Adrienne Rich, *On Lies, Secrets, and Silence: Selected Prose 1966–1978* (New York: W. W. Norton, 1979), 123.

9. Kumin, *Always Beginning*, 75.

10. Kumin, "The Ancient Lady Poets," in *The Long Marriage* (New York and London: W. W. Norton, 2002), 112.

11. Matters of poetic craft are often discussed in Maxine Kumin's published interviews. Enid Shomer's detailed interview with Kumin appears in *Always Beginning*, and Steven Ratiner's interview, "A New Life in the Barn," appears in Steven Ratiner, ed., *Giving Their Word: Conversations with Contemporary Poets* (Amherst: University of Massachusetts Press, 2002), 129–145.

12. Kumin, "A Sense of Place," 172.

13. See "A Way of Staying Sane," as well as Kumin's address to the Sandhill Writers' Conference in May of 1998, titled "Premonitory Shiver," reprinted in *Always Beginning.*

14. Ibid.

Stanley Kunitz

THE LAYERS

Stanley Kunitz

C ommercial Street in Provincetown, Massachusetts, takes a sharp left-angled turn as it runs past the Coast Guard Station and winds into the West End, paralleling the Bay. Here the busy shops that give Commercial Street its name yield to cedar-shake cottages, boat slips, and that outermost reach, the spit of land that separates Provincetown from the Atlantic Ocean, the location where Henry David Thoreau said a man could stand "and put all of America behind him." Stanley Kunitz's garden, with its profusion of blooms and dancing array of colors is enough to pull any visitor's eyes away – even from the hypnotic sea. Located at 32 Commercial Street behind a wrought-iron gate and terraced in levels running down to the house, the garden literally stops people in their tracks. Although small gardens and window boxes filled with flowers pop up with regularity along Provincetown's narrow streets, this abundant and vividly layered collection of perennials is like no other in the village.

When Kunitz bought the property in 1962, the front yard was like most in this village by the sea: a sand dune. Moreover, the lot ran in a steep grade down to a two-story gray bungalow. Kunitz decided that if he was to create a garden he'd have to terrace it, so he constructed a series of tiers, bordered by low brick

NOTE: In mid-May 2006, shortly before this book went to press, Stanley Kunitz died at the age of one hundred. While the afterword and acknowledgments reflect this fact, I've allowed his chapter to unfold as it took place. On the day Kunitz died I overheard a colleague remark, with a mixture of sorrow and admiration, "He cast a long shadow." I prefer to think he cast a long light.

walls, rising progressively up from the house to the street. The terraces are of varying widths, each containing its own palette of colors, each blooming at staggered intervals during the seasons, an undulating wave of color.

Kunitz built the soil from equal amounts of sand, peat moss, and compost, adding seaweed and sea grasses that he collected at low tide. He labored for two summers to prepare the space, and his efforts to enrich, maintain, and renew the garden have consumed the daylight hours of dozens of summers. Provincetown insiders love to tell the story of tourists stopping to ask the slight, white-haired man working in the garden the secret of his success, unaware that they are speaking to one of the great masters of poetry.

"People stop and go 'Ooh' and 'Ah' and he says 'Thank you,' 'Thank you,' but does not talk. He often tells them he is the hired hand," or so the story goes.

Excavations, layers, a careful rebuilding and enriching of the soil is a process that might serve as an apt metaphor for his poems which are, by his own description, slow to evolve, much worked over, long ripening. In a writing career that has spanned more than seventy-five years he has published ten volumes of his own poems, a number of translations of Russian poets, a dozen essays and reviews – garnering in the steadily evolving process a Pulitzer Prize, a National Book Award, and the honor of being named poet laureate twice, the second time at the age of ninety-five.

Although not a nature poet, Kunitz feels

a considerable attachment to place. My work has always been associated with my habitat and especially with my gardens. I cannot separate them. I'm not content merely to be a reporter of the scene. What I am looking for is to somehow come in touch with the mystery of existence itself.

Born in Worcester, Massachusetts, in 1905, Kunitz was the child of immigrant parents from Lithuania. His father, Solomon Kunitz, committed suicide in a public park just six weeks before Stanley's birth. His mother, Yetta, left with a failing dress-manufacturing business, a baby and two older children, was so embittered by the act that she stripped the house of any reminders of her husband and forbade the children to ever speak his name. The trauma haunted Kunitz's childhood, interrupting his sleep patterns and affecting his biological rhythms. For years Kunitz has written after dinner, long into the night, rarely going to bed until the early hours of the morning. He admits that he "fights sleep as long as possible," but also believes he is, by nature, a "night-bird" and that if he spends the daylight hours tiring his body with physical exertion, the night-time opens more readily into imagination's territory, the mysterious state of consciousness where poems are born.

When Kunitz was eight his mother successfully reestablished the dressmaking business and married a second time. Although this gentle, scholarly man, in Kunitz's words, "showed me the ways of tenderness and affection," he died six years later, doubling the impact of the loss of a father.

The double loss of the father marked Kunitz's poetry as surely as his life. Not only did the search for the lost father sear through the images and lines of his poems, he became, early on, a father figure for many young poets. He, who had no mentor, became the mentor par excellence, a truth not lost on Kunitz himself.

> Oh yes, I think that since I had no mentor I realized how important mentoring and a community of poets can be. I experienced a long search for someone who could stand as a representative of the search for one's identity; who could ascertain who one was and how one could create art out of that. It's not surprising that I tried to

shorten that search for others, younger poets, some of
them my students, many of them women – who carry
the authentic passion of their lives and causes.

FATHER AND SON

Now in the suburbs and the falling light
I followed him, and now down sandy road
Whiter than bone-dust, through the sweet
Curdle to fields, where the plums
Dropped with their load of ripeness, one by one.
Mile after mile I followed, with skimming feet,
After the secret master of my blood,
Him steeped in the odor of ponds, whose indomitable love
Kept me in chains. Strode years; stretched into bird;
Raced through the sleeping country where I was young,
The silence unrolling before me as I came,
The night nailed like an orange to my brow.

How should I tell him my fable and the fears,
How bridge the chasm in a casual tone,
Saying, "The house, the stucco one you built,
We lost. Sister married and went from home,
And nothing comes back, it's strange, from where she goes.
I lived on a hill that had too many rooms:
Light we could make, but not enough of warmth,
And when the light failed, I climbed under the hill.
The papers are delivered every day;
I am alone and never shed a tear."

At the water's edge, where the smothering ferns lifted
Their arms, "Father!" I cried, "Return! You know
The way. I'll wipe the mudstains from your clothes;
No trace, I promise, will remain. Instruct

Your son, whirling between two wars,
In the Gemara of your gentleness,
For I would be a child to those who mourn
And brother to the foundlings of the field
And friend of innocence and all bright eyes.
O teach me how to work and keep me kind."

Among the turtles and the lilies he turned to me
The white ignorant hollow of his face.

Always an excellent student, Kunitz went to Harvard in 1923; there he compiled a sterling record, graduating summa cum laude in 1926. He took a master's degree in 1927, anticipating staying on at Harvard as a member of the faculty, but a different fate awaited.

I was told indirectly through the head of the English department that Anglo Saxons would resent being taught English by a Jew, even by a Jew with a summa cum laude. That shook my world. It seemed to me such a cruel and wanton rejection that I turned away from academic life completely. After I left Harvard I had no real contact with universities for almost twenty years.[1]

He returned, instead, to Worcester, taking a job as a reporter on the local newspaper. Other editorial work followed, compiling and editing reference books. In 1930 he published his first volume of poetry, *Intellectual Things*.

In the years that followed he married twice, each time settling with his wife in the country. With Helen Pearce he tried to survive in the midst of the Depression on a one-hundred-acre farm in Connecticut, cultivating food for his own use and herbs as commercial crops. In 1939 he shifted his residence to an old stone house in New Hope, Pennsylvania, where with his second wife, Eleanor Evans, he raised chickens, planted trees, and landed a job with a Bronx-based publisher who specialized in biographical dictionaries.

"One evening Ted Roethke drove down to New Hope from Lafayette and knocked on my door, unannounced, with a copy of *Intellectual Things* in his hand," Kunitz recalls. "It astonished me that this big, shambling stranger knew my poems by heart."[2] Theodore Roethke and Kunitz became good friends; each appreciated the warmth the other provided – a breaking of a writer's isolation – and they shared some poetic and psychological common denominators, including familiarity and love of plants, flowers, and growing things, and the loss of a father at an early age. Years later Kunitz was to say of of this friendship,

> I think that for the rest of our lives we really had a sense of true fellowship, comradeship, even when we were at opposite ends of the continent. . . . We were helpful to each other in a way that two poets can be who share some of the same values and loves. And to me he was always the most important poet of my generation, even when he was unknown.[3]

Just before his thirty-eighth birthday, in 1943, Kunitz was drafted into the U.S. Army, "as a non-affiliated pacifist, with moral scruples against bearing arms. My understanding with the draft board was that I would be assigned to a service unit, such as the Medical Corps," Kunitz says.

> Instead, the papers on my status got lost or were never delivered, and I was shuttled for three years from camp to camp, doing KP duty most of the time or digging latrines. A combination of pneumonia, scarlet fever, and just downright humiliation almost did me in. While I was still in uniform, *Passport to the War*, my bleakest book, was published, but I was scarcely aware of the event. It seemed to sink without a trace.[4]

Shortly before his discharge from the service, he was contacted by the president of Bennington College to replace Roethke who had suffered one of his most severe manic episodes and insisted that Kunitz substitute for him. Although his tenure at Bennington was brief (he left abruptly after he was chastised for organizing a student protest when a student was about to be unfairly expelled), Bennington marked the first academic stop on a long journey into teaching. He and his wife moved briefly when he accepted an upstate New York teaching position. Despite the birth of a daughter, Gretchen, they separated in 1952, and Kunitz left for Europe on a two-year traveling fellowship.

After a teaching stint at the University of Washington (again replacing Theodore Roethke), Kunitz came to New York in 1956 where he began cultivating friendships with a group of abstract expressionist painters: Mark Rothko, Franz Kline, Philip Guston, Robert Motherwell. He also met Elise Asher, an artist who had begun as a poet, but had turned to painting as well. She, too, was recovering from a failed marriage, had a young daughter, had lost a parent at any early age, and moved easily among a wide arc of painters in Greenwich Village. Within a year they married, settling first on West Twelfth Street and summering in a shack on the beach among Provincetown's large community of visual artists. Subsequently, they moved down the block to a more spacious apartment on West Twelfth when Kunitz began to teach in the graduate writing program at Columbia University and bought the bungalow on Provincetown's West End, where they created basement work studios.

Kunitz feels a real affinity with painters and considers himself "lucky to be married into their world."

> I envy them because there is so much physical satisfaction in the actual work of painting and sculpture. I'm a physical being and resent this sedentary business of sitting at one's desk and moving only one's wrists. I pace. I speak my poems. I get very kinetic when I'm working.

But the artist can also pay a heavy price: he can sacrifice too much, or be poisoned by ambition, or carry too heavy a load of grief. We've seen examples of that kind of destruction in poets and painters in our time. That's one of the things I tried to explore in my poem about my good friend, the painter Mark Rothko, shortly after he committed suicide.

THE ARTIST

His paintings grew darker every year.
They filled the walls, they filled the room;
eventually they filled his world –
all but the ravishment.
When voices faded, he would rush to hear
the scratched soul of Mozart
endless in gyre.
Back and forth, back and forth,
he paced the paint-smeared floor,
diminishing in size each time he turned,
trapped in his monumental void,
raving against his adversaries.
At last he took a knife in his hand
and slashed an exit for himself
between the frames of his tall scenery.
Through the holes of his tattered universe
the first innocence and the light
came pouring in.

In 1957, at a New York party bringing together poets and painters, Kunitz ran into Richard Wilbur – and there the fortuitous encounter Wilbur described earlier took place. Kunitz remembers the meeting vividly: "Dick was a friend of my work," he observes, underscoring each word carefully. So the poet who had not published a book for fourteen years, released his third volume, *Selected Poems, 1928–1958*, which promptly won the Pulitzer Prize. The authority of Kunitz's poetic voice, its moral gravity and measured dignity, registers in many of the poems in this collection and is superceded, perhaps, only by the second collection of selected poems, *The Poems of Stanley Kunitz 1928–1978*. Within that collection is the poem "The Layers," whose haunting conclusion is among the most oft-quoted passages in contemporary verse.

> *In my darkest night,*
> *when the moon was covered*
> *and I roamed through the wreckage,*
> *a nimbus-clouded voice*
> *directed me:*
> *"Live in the layers,*
> *not on the litter."*
> *Though I lack the art*
> *to decipher it,*
> *no doubt the next chapter*
> *in my book of transformations*
> *is already written*
> *I am not done with my changes.*

As Kunitz wheeled into the next chapter in his book of transformations, he entered a period his friend and editor Peter Davison called "his great old age," a time marked by a distinguished teaching career; the mentoring of a whole new generation of poets including Michael Ryan, Marie Howe, Susan Mitchell, and Louise Glück; important translation work, particularly of Russian poets Akhmatova, Yevtushenko, and Voznesensky; and the founding of two important resource centers for artists. The Fine Arts Work Center in Provincetown, which houses the Stanley Kunitz Common Room, was founded in 1968 and offers long-term residencies to artists, poets, and fiction writers. Kunitz also helped found Poets House, a forty-thousand volume public poetry library and reading room on Spring Street in New York, where poets congregate for book fairs, public readings, and panel discussions. Clearly, his concern with helping to create and support a community of artists and writers derives from the isolation of his early and middle years.

> Art withers without fellowship. I recall how grievously I missed the sense of a community in my own youth. In a typical American city or town poets are strangers. If our society provided a more satisfying cultural climate, a more spontaneous and generous environment, we shouldn't need to install specialized writing workshops in the universities or endow places like Yaddo or Mac-Dowell or Provincetown. In Provincetown we invite a number of young writers and visual artists from all parts of the country to live at the Center for an extended period of time, working freely in association. Our policy is not to impose a pattern on them, but to let them create their own. In practice, instead of becoming competitive, they soon want to talk to one another about their work problems, they begin to share their manuscripts and paintings, they arrange their own group sessions, they meet visiting writers and artists and consult with them, if they are so inclined. Most who come for the seven-month term are loath to leave. Many of them stay on as residents of the town.[5]

Kunitz often remarks that he learns as much as he gives in his teaching and mentoring and that his association with the resource centers brings him closer to new generations of writers than he ever was to his own generation. At the dedication of the common room bearing his name, his former student, the poet Marie Howe, confirmed that his trust in a new generation of poets is neither misplaced or unreciprocated.

"No true teaching happens without love," she began.

Stanley once said, "I dream of an art so transparent that you can look through it and see the world." And he taught us to love this world, to learn the names of the rocks and plants and animals. He taught us that we are not alone, that the world is noisy with a breathing chain of being, a web in which we live, and that every molecule of it matters.

He taught us to love the places we had come from, places many of us were trying to forget, Pittsburgh or Rochester or the streets of New York, the very meadows and backyards we had struggled to get out of once and for all. He taught us to love that geography, the "testing-trees" of our own childhood, the original dirt and water and matter of our first lives.

And in that way he taught us to love our own stories, what we had hidden, what we had been ashamed of. He taught us to turn into those obsessions that haunted us and hurt us, to turn into their "deeper dark." And we looked at his own work and saw that he had done so, and that he had made of those turnings, poetry. And we took courage and tried.[6]

I first met Stanley Kunitz in October of 1984; he had come to read his poems at Mercyhurst College just thirty minutes north of the college in western Pennsylvania where I was teaching. Several of us were invited to attend the reading and meet the poet afterwards. Although not yet the recipient of the many honors bestowed on him in his nineties, he had already entered his "great old age," when the power of his poems seemed to increase exponentially, poem to poem, volume to volume, and when his generosity to younger writers – particularly women poets – created admiration in many quarters. Perhaps five feet six inches tall, with an athletic, rolling gait, Kunitz came onto the auditorium stage flanked by two exceedingly tall Sisters of Mercy. He wore a checked shirt, knit tie, a modest sport jacket and slacks, and his hair, sparse on top, flowing into long and fluffy sideburns, seemed to surround him like a halo. He stood quietly while one of the towering nuns introduced him. Raising one hand to quiet the applause that erupted from the crowd, he stepped behind the lectern, opened his book, and began to read the poem "The Testing-Tree" – his voice rising into fiery incantation, as he implored:

> *In a murderous time*
> *the heart breaks and breaks*
> *and lives by breaking.*
> *It is necessary to go*
> *through dark and deeper dark*
> *and not to turn.*

He read for forty-five minutes without a break and with very little "patter" prefacing the poems. I don't remember hearing even a cough breaking the sound of that voice, though I believe many were moved to tears.

Fifteen years later I saw Kunitz again fill a college auditorium, this time at Smith College where his reading generated standing-room-only conditions. He had been newly named United States Poet Laureate. The years had deepened the wit and wisdom in his face; he had less hair, though the mustache that balances on the tip of his upper lip was still full. The voice remained the same: fiery, measured, rhythmic, rising into a crescendo when he read perhaps his best-known poem, "The Wellfleet Whale."

THE WELLFLEET WHALE

A few summers ago, on Cape Cod, a whale foundered on the beach, a sixty-three-foot finback whale. When the tide went out, I approached him. He was lying there, in monstrous desolation, making the most

*terrifying noises – rumbling – groaning. I put my hands on his flanks
and I could feel the life inside him. And while I was standing there,
suddenly he opened his eye. It was a big, red, cold eye, and it was
staring directly at me. A shudder of recognition passed between us.
Then the eye closed forever. I've been thinking about whales ever since.*

– Journal Entry

I

*You have your language too,
    an eerie medley of clicks
        and hoots and trills,
location-notes and love calls,
    whistles and grunts. Occasionally,
        it's like furniture being smashed,
or the creaking of a mossy door,
    sounds that all melt into a liquid
        song with endless variations,
as if to compensate
    for the vast loneliness of the sea.
        Sometimes a disembodied voice
breaks in, as if from distant reefs,
    and it's as much as one can bear
        to listen to its long mournful cry,
a sorrow without name, both more
    and less than human. It drags
        across the ear like a record
running down.*

2

*No wind. No waves. No clouds.
    Only the whisper of the tide,
        as it withdrew, stroking the shore,
a lazy drift of gulls overhead,
    and tiny points of light*

bubbling in the channel.
It was the tag-end of summer.
From the harbor's mouth
*   you coasted into sight,*
flashing news of your advent,
*   the crescent of your dorsal fin*
*   clipping the diamonded surface.*
We cheered at the sign of your greatness
*   when the black barrel of your head*
*   erupted, ramming the water,*
and you flowered for us
*   in the jet of your spouting.*

3
All afternoon you swam
*   tirelessly round the bay,*
*   with such an easy motion,*
the slightest downbeat of your tail,
*   an almost imperceptible*
*   undulation of your flippers,*
you seemed like something poured,
*   not driven; you seemed*
*   to marry grace with power.*
And when you bounded into air,
*   slapping your flukes*
*   we thrilled to look upon*
pure energy incarnate
*   as nobility of form.*
*   You seemed to ask of us*
not sympathy, or love,
*   or understanding,*
*   but awe and wonder.*

That night we watched you
*   swimming in the moon.*

Your back was molten silver.
We guessed your silent passage
   by the phosphorescence in your wake.
      At dawn we found you stranded on the rocks.

   4
There came a boy and a man
   and yet other men running, and two
      schoolgirls in yellow halters
and a housewife bedecked
   with curlers, and whole families in beach
      buggies with assorted yelping dogs.
The tide was almost out.
   We could walk around you,
      as you heaved deeper into the shoal,
crushed by your own weight,
   collapsing into yourself,
      your flippers and your flukes
quivering, your blowhole
   spasmodically bubbling, roaring.
      In the pit of your gaping mouth
you bared your fringework of baleen,
   a thicket of horned bristles.
      When the Curator of Mammals
arrived from Boston
   to take samples of your blood
      you were already oozing from below.
Somebody had carved his initials
   in your flank. Hunters of souvenirs
      had peeled off strips of your skin,
a membrane as thin as paper.
   You were blistered and cracked by the sun.
      The gulls had been pecking at you.
The sound you made was a hoarse and fitful bleating.
What drew us, like a magnet, to your dying?

You made a bond between us,
the keepers of the nightfall watch,
who gathered in a ring around you
boozing in the bonfire light.
Toward dawn we shared with you
your hour of desolation,
the huge lingering passion
of your unearthly outcry,
as you swung your blind head
toward us and laboriously opened
a bloodshot, glistening eye,
in which we swam with terror and recognition.

5

Voyager, chief of the pelagic world,
you brought with you the myth
of another country, dimly remembered,
where flying reptiles
lumbered over the steaming marshes
and trumpeting thunder lizards
wallowed in the reeds.
While empires rose and fell on land,
your nation breasted the open main,
rocked in the consoling rhythm
of the tides. Which ancestor first plunged
head-down through the zones of colored twilight
to scour the bottom of the dark?
You ranged the North Atlantic track
from Port-of-Spain to Baffin Bay,
edging between the ice-floes
through the fat of summer,
lob-tailing, breaching, sounding,
grazing in the pastures of the sea
on krill-rich orange plankton
crackling with life.

You prowled down the continental shelf,
guided by the sun and stars
and the taste of alluvial silt
on your way southward
to the warm lagoons,
the tropic of desire,
where the lovers lie belly to belly
in the rub and nuzzle of their sporting;
and you turned, like a god in exile,
out of your wide primeval element,
delivered to the mercy of time.

Master of the whale-roads,
let the white wings of the gulls
spread out their cover.
You have become like us,
disgraced and mortal.

It was that voice I heard on the phone in January of 2004 – strong, deliberate, rhythmic. On two previous occasions in early winter I had arranged to visit Kunitz at his apartment in New York City. Each time, major Nor'easters had swept across the eastern seaboard, making travel impossible. Ever accommodating, he had agreed, with the help of his literary assistant, Genine Lentine, to do a phone interview. Since it is hard for him to hear on the phone, I knew I needed to confine myself to crucial questions. When I asked him how he would describe the role of the poet as witness, there was a long pause. I could hear him thinking. He cleared his throat several times and then replied in one seamless paragraph:

Poets in any culture inherit a common tradition. What makes them separate and distinctive is the use they make of their own past, which cannot be the same as anybody else's. My first sense of what it meant to be a poet in the modern world was that it required a search for my own identity. To ascertain who I was and then to bear witness to it is at the heart of my poetry. Sometimes I feel perturbed that I've written so few poems on political themes, particularly on the causes that agitate me. But then I realize that being a poet at all in the modern world is a political act.[7]

In mid-July of 2004 I was invited to Provincetown to speak with Kunitz once again. Although he had lost Elise in March, he had returned to Provincetown, as was their custom, to stay from late June until the middle of October. He was working with Genine on his "summer project," compiling thoughts about the garden into a big multi-subject bound manuscript that would ultimately be fashioned into a book.

The day was sunny, the light dancing on the bay all the way out to Long Point Light. I let myself in through the wrought-iron gate, into that enclosed garden ablaze with lemon and ruby daylilies. Stanley sat in an upholstered armchair in a front alcove of the living room. He wore khaki pants and a checked shirt, and he raised a hand high in greeting. Sun, filtering through the drapes, made his skin almost translucent.

Paintings in bright, primary colors covered the walls, a number of them belonging to the recognizable series Elise Asher created to accompany Kunitz's poem "The Long Boat." What Provincetown natives call a "Portuguese fireplace" – an open wood-burning stove – sat on a raised brick hearth in the middle of the living room floor and, at the other end of the room, a long sturdy table held the early preparations for a birthday party. The floor, unpainted wood, was barefoot-smooth, with a little sand caught in the cracks between the wide boards.

Together we leafed through my copy of his Collected Poems, with Kunitz offering witty or reflective sidebars to individual poems and pointing emphatically with his long tapered fingers to particular favorites. He paused at an early poem, tapping the page, saying the words of the title very deliberately: "I Dreamed I Was Old." "That," he said, his moustache twitching slightly, "seems ludicrous now."

Genine showed me the notebook on the garden they were compiling together, a big book, fat with entries sectioned off into tabbed categories. Two photos of Kunitz bookend the text: the frontispiece shows the poet bending toward the terraced garden, preparing to work – his cane held as if it were a gardening tool; the final image, shot from the rear, depicts the poet returning to the house, two large buckets of dirt in hand, one swinging jauntily behind his back.

A poet in her own right, as well as Kunitz's literary assistant, Genine carries a quiet authority – liberally salted with joie de vivre (not unlike her boss). When I observed that she was probably too young to have been one of Kunitz's students at Columbia, she nodded.

"That's right, I was not a student of Stanley's. But he is certainly a teacher to me. His capacity for listening is immense and that is one of the greatest gifts a teacher can offer."

I knew the question I most wanted to ask of the man who has lived – thus far – through the tenure of fifteen presidents.

B: You've described your voice as elegiac.
K: (*leaning forward*) Yes.
B: And you've described our age as a "murderous time."
K: (*forcefully*) Yes.
B: I'm wondering, then, if you have faith in the role of the poet in our time.
K: (*looking at me intently*) I have absolute conviction about poetry at any time.

Suddenly the room was very bright, as if lit from within.

ENDNOTES

1. Michael Ryan, "Periodicity" in *Interviews and Encounters with Stanley Kunitz*, Stanley Moss, ed. (New York: Sheep Meadow Press, 1993), 61. This book, coupled with an earlier collection of poems and recollections, titled, *A Celebration* (New York: Sheep Meadow Press, 1986, reissued 1996) are excellent sources of information on Kunitz's life, art, and teaching.

2. Stanley Kunitz, "Interview with Chris Busa," in *Next-to-Last Things: New Poems and Essays* (Boston: Atlantic-Little Brown, 1985), 92.

3. David Lupher, "Language Surprised" in *Interviews and Encounters with Stanley Kunitz*, 8.

4. Busa, 93.

5. Ibid., 108.

6. Marie Howe, "A Tribute to Stanley Kunitz," in *Interviews and Encounters with Stanley Kunitz*, xv. Another useful profile assessing Stanley Kunitz in his ninety-eighth year is Dana Goodyear's "The Gardener," in the *New Yorker*, September 1, 2003.

7. That choosing to be a poet in the modern world constitutes a political act is an idea Kunitz explores in many interviews and something he reiterates in the "Reflections" section of his *Collected Poems*. (New York: W. W. Norton, 2000).

Afterword

To EXPLORE THE LIVES and work of Donald Hall, Richard Wilbur, Maxine Kumin, and Stanley Kunitz is to face the temptation of converting them into legends. After all, the example of their excellence and sustained achievement places them in that rare position of having blazed a literary path through much of twentieth-century history.

Veneration has its price, however. Almost thirty years ago, Donald Hall cautioned against its dangers by offering a striking series of portraits of four poets who were among the primary movers and shakers of his youth. *Remembering Poets* (1978) profiles Hall's encounters with T. S. Eliot, Robert Frost, Ezra Pound, and Dylan Thomas as they neared the end of their lives; Hall pictures writers whose wit and brilliance contended proportionally with vanity, alcoholism, and fame, as well as with the prejudices of time and place. His was no sentimental tribute, no suspending of poetic genius in amber, preserved for the ages.

During the two-year period I spent compiling this book, the poets were hardly sitting still for tributes, even if I had been tempted to construct them. Kunitz is perhaps the primary example of a poet who worked productively into very old age. He won a National Book Award at the age of ninety, was named poet laureate at the age of ninety-five, and published (with Genine Lentine) *The Wild Braid: A Poet Reflects on a Century in the Garden* a few months before his one-hundredth birthday. Richard Wilbur published his *Collected Poems* and won the prestigious Ruth Lilly Award. Maxine Kumin published a new collection of poems titled *Jack, and Other New Poems* and won the Harvard Arts Medal. Donald Hall published *The Best Day The Worst Day*, a memoir of his life with Jane Kenyon; in June 2006 he was appointed United States Poet Laureate. None waited to be preserved in amber.

The world of contemporary poetry has often been described as a "village," a small enclave where sooner or later a poet bumps into every other poet, with competitive or cooperative consequences. Although some of the connections among Hall, Wilbur, Kumin and Kunitz might be anticipated, given their commonalities of history, educational experience, and love of New England, their bonds are deeper than simple intersections of time and place. Maxine Kumin may have evoked those bonds most memorably in her "random lines" to Stanley Kunitz.

FOR STANLEY, SOME LINES AT RANDOM

You, Sir, with the red snippers
who twice saw Halley's comet fly,
you, who can identify
Coprinus, *chanterelle and sundry*
others of the damp-woods fleet,
whose broadside "The Long Boat"
produced on handmade paper
woven from your discards –
here, *the delivery boy declared*
is Mr. Kunitz's laundry –
hangs in my study,

it's forty years since I, a guest
in your Provincetown retreat
arose from what you said
had once been e. e. cummings's bed
to breakfast on an omelet

fat with choice boletuses
that had erupted in
your three-tiered garden,
perhaps under one of your dahlias
the size of a dinner plate,
a garden that took decades to create.

Luck of the alphabet,
since 1961 we've leaned
against each other, spine
on spine, positioned thus.
Upright or slant, long may we stand
on shelves dusted or not
to be taken up by hands
that cherish us.

Ultimately, beyond the lives of the poets lies the force of the work itself. Poems are acts of connection – seeking communion with a reader, a listener, who can take the poem in, be calmed, transported, or challenged to action.

This communion is the sustained and sustaining light embedded in the poems of Donald Hall, Richard Wilbur, Maxine Kumin, and Stanley Kunitz. It is as complicated, as resonant, and as enduring as our capacity to receive it.

Selected Readings

Donald Hall, Richard Wilbur, Maxine Kumin, and Stanley Kunitz have written many chapters of their own life experience in poems, essays, and memoirs spanning more than five decades. They will augment and enrich the portraits in this book for any reader interested in exploring them.

DONALD HALL

String Too Short to be Saved: Recollections of Summers on a New England Farm. Boston: David R. Godine, Publisher, 1960, Reprint; 1981.

Remembering Poets: Reminiscences and Opinions. New York: Harper & Row, 1977, 1978.

Kicking the Leaves. New York: Harper & Row, 1978.

Seasons at Eagle Pond. Boston and New York: Houghton Mifflin Company, 1987.

Life Work. Boston: Beacon Press, 1993.

Without: Poems. Boston & New York: Houghton Mifflin Company, 1998.

The Painted Bed: Poems. Boston & New York: Houghton Mifflin Company, 2002.

RICHARD WILBUR

Ceremony. New York: Harcourt Brace & Company, 1950.

Things of this World. New York: Harcourt Brace & Company, 1956.

Advice to a Prophet. New York: Harcourt Brace & Company, 1961.

Walking to Sleep. New York: Harcourt Brace & Company, 1969.

New and Collected Poems. New York: Harcourt Brace & Company, 1988.

Mayflies. New York, San Diego, London: Harcourt, Brace & Company, 2000.

Responses. New York and London: Harcourt, Brace, Jovanovich, 1976. Reprinted, with additional material, Ashland, Oregon: Story Line Press, 2000.

MAXINE KUMIN

The Retrieval System. New York: Penguin Books, 1978.

In Deep: Country Essays. New York: Viking, 1987.

Women, Animals, and Vegetables: Essays and Stories. New York: W. W. Norton, 1994.

Selected Poems, 1960–1990. New York and London: W. W. Norton, 1997.

Always Beginning: Essays on a Life in Poetry. Port Townsend, Washington, Copper Canyon Press, 2000.

Inside the Halo and Beyond. New York and London: W. W. Norton, 2000.

The Long Marriage. New York and London: W. W. Norton, 2002.

STANLEY KUNITZ

Selected Poems, 1928–1958. Boston: Atlantic–Little, Brown, 1958.

The Testing Tree: Poems. Boston: Atlantic–Little, Brown, 1971.

The Coat without a Seam: Sixty Poems, 1930–1972. Northampton, Massachusetts: Gehenna Press, 1974.

A Kind of Order, A Kind of Folly: Essays and Conversations. Boston: Atlantic–Little, Brown, 1975.

The Wellfleet Whale and Companion Poems. New York: Sheep Meadow Press, 1983.

Next-to-Last Things: New Poems and Essays. Boston: Atlantic–Little, Brown, 1985.

Passing Through: The Later Poems. New York and London: W. W. Norton, 1995.

The Collected Poems. New York and London: W. W. Norton, 2000.

Acknowledgments

My primary thanks go to Donald Hall, Richard Wilbur, Maxine Kumin, and in memoriam, Stanley Kunitz, who, despite their being previously interviewed on dozens of occasions, allowed me to believe I was asking three or four original questions. Without their enthusiastic participation and painstaking care with the finished product, these essays might never have come to light.

I'm deeply grateful for a generous grant from the John Anson Kittredge Foundation at Harvard in support of the publication of this book.

Jane Garrett and Lynn Walterick, whose superb editorial counsel is unique and abiding, provided advice and practical support when I most needed it.

Genine Lentine, Stanley Kunitz's literary assistant and a poet in her own right, was crucial in arranging and facilitating my conversations with Stanley. I don't know if I'd agree with a journalist from the *New Yorker* who suggested that Genine and Stanley were "joined at the hip," but they certainly were joined at the heart.

Heartfelt thanks to David R. Godine, the gold standard in independent book publishing, who liked this book well enough to publish it and who continues to believe that how a book is made is as important as what it contains.

It was at Barry Moser's urging, one wintry afternoon more than two years ago, that I screwed up the courage to approach the four brightest stars in my literary firmament. Not only did Barry insist that everybody had the right, even the obligation, to write his or her "dream book," but offered to collaborate with me by providing engravings to illustrate the book. We traveled together to visit several poets, Barry sketching and photographing them and their landscapes while I conducted the interviews; later, we ate enormous breakfasts, talking excitedly about the results. I couldn't have invented a better creative companion. To you, Barry: *con affettuosi ringraziamenti.*

PERMISSIONS ACKNOWLEDGMENTS

Donald Hall: "Weeds and Peonies, " from *Without: Poems*. Copyright © 1998 by Donald Hall. "Mount Kearsarge," "My Son, My Executioner," and "Names of Horses," from *Old and New Poems*. Copyright © 1990 by Donald Hall. Reprinted by permission of Houghton Mifflin Company. All rights reserved.

Richard Wilbur: "Cottage Street" and "Love Calls Us to the Things of This World," from *New and Collected Poems*. Copyright © 1988 by Richard Wilbur. Reprinted by permission of Harcourt, Inc.

Maxine Kumin: "Morning Swim" and "How It Is," from *Selected Poems 1960–1990*. Copyright © 1998 by Maxine Kumin. "Want," from *The Long Marriage*. Copyright © 2002 by Maxine Kumin. "Some Lines at Random," from *Jack and Other New Poems*. Copyright © 2005 by Maxine Kumin. Reprinted by permission of W. W. Norton, Inc.

Stanley Kunitz: "The Testing Tree" and "The Layers," and "The Wellfleet Whale," from *The Collected Poems*. Copyright © 2000 by Stanley Kunitz. Reprinted by permission of W. W. Norton, Inc.

Gary Snyder: "How Poetry Comes to Me," from *No Nature: New and Selected Poems*. Copyright © 1992 by Gary Snyder. Reprinted by permission of Pantheon Books, a division of Random House.

ABOUT THE AUTHOR

JEANNE BRAHAM, *the author of four books on American arts and letters, writes frequently about contemporary American poets. She is the founding editor of Heatherstone Press, a publisher of poetry chapbooks, and serves as the poetry editor of* New England Watershed *magazine.*

ABOUT THE ARTIST

BARRY MOSER *is a native of Tennessee who makes his home in western Massachusetts. Currently on the Smith College faculty in the art department, he also serves as Printer to the College. His work is in collections and libraries around the world. His 1999 edition of the King James Bible has received international attention and acclaim.*

A NOTE ON THE TYPE

THE LIGHT WITHIN THE LIGHT *has been set in Monotype Dante, a face designed by the renowned scholar, typographer, and printer, Giovanni Mardersteig for use at his Officina Bodoni in Verona, Italy. The types were cut in the 1950s by Charles Malin, the legendary French punchcutter whose first work for Mardersteig was to recut the fragile Bodoni characters used in the Officina's publication of the works of Gabriele D'Annunzio. Malin's collaboration with Mardersteig produced a series of handsome faces over the span of twenty-five years – Griffo and Zeno among them – and would later produce the Pacioli titling series, but Dante can justly be called their masterpiece. The Dante type takes as its models the Italian types of the fifteenth century, but the deftness of Mardersteig's cutting and the brilliance of Malin's cutting save the type from the excessive refinement that limits the usefulness of many faces cut for private presses. ☙ The display type is Waters Titling, a type based on the calligraphic work of the noted American lettering artist, Julian Waters.*

DESIGN BY BARRY MOSER AND CARL W. SCARBROUGH